Education
for the
Earth

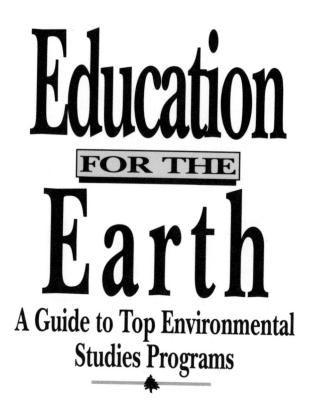

Education

FOR THE

Earth

A Guide to Top Environmental Studies Programs

*Published in cooperation with
the Alliance for Environmental Education*

 **Peterson's Guides**
Princeton, New Jersey

Library of Congress Cataloging-in-Publication Data

Education for the Earth : a guide to top environmental studies programs / Alliance for Environmental Education.
     p.   cm.
    Includes bibliographical references and index.
    ISBN 1-56079-164-0
    1. Environmental sciences—study and teaching (higher)—United States. 2. Environmental sciences vocational guidance. I. Alliance for Environmental Education.
GE80.E33   1993
363.7'071'173—dc20
                            92-33025

Composition and design by Peterson's Guides

Cover design by Greg Wuttke

Printed in the United States of America

10 9 8 7 6 5 4 3 2 1

Printed on recycled paper.

Contents

Contents

Environmental Studies

Natural Resources Management

Foreword

Steven C. Kussmann
Chairman, Alliance for Environmental Education

Did you know that if Americans recycled all of their Sunday newspapers, we could save 500,000 trees each week or 26 million every year?"

The fact that a statement like this is found on the inside flap of a cereal box is indicative of the high level of awareness there is about environmental protection in our society. The environment is big business. Today many corporations are employing a vice president–level environmental liaison. For certain, environmental specialization for all professions is on the horizon. No matter what field of endeavor one chooses, there is little doubt that career preparation in today's world will include concern for the environment.

But how can one find out how to prepare for the environmental career opportunities that exist today? How can one plan the best path into graduate-level environmental training? This guide provides a starting point for discovering the answers to these questions. The only guide to undergraduate environmental education programs in the United States, it gives practical advice about where the professional opportunities lie and what colleges and universities are best prepared to help students pursue them.

Acknowledgments

We give sincere thanks to the *Education for the Earth* advisory board, which formed the philosophy and purpose for the guide and established the criteria for identifying leading environmental studies programs in the United States. This board included Shirley Ireton, National Science Teachers Association; Harvey Olem, The Terrene Institute; Jack Padalino, Pocono Environmental Education Center; Bradley Smith, U.S. Environmental Protection Agency; Keith Wheeler, Adirondack Park Visitor Interpretive Center; and Brett Wright, George Mason University.

In addition, we are grateful to the individuals who prepared the essays for the CareerWatch section of this guide: Kenneth T. Derr, Chevron Corporation; Robert L. Herbst, Tennessee Valley Authority; David V. McCalley, University of Northern Iowa; and Jay D. Hair, National Wildlife Federation.

Special thanks must also go to the participating schools for their cooperation during the survey process and in particular their diligence in completing the wonderful descriptions of their programs.

Finally, credit is due to Alliance staff members Tom Benjamin, for his coordination of the project, and Jan Hunt, for her editorial assistance.

How to Use This Book

I t is likely you are reading this book because you are a student (or the parent of one) who is strongly interested in environmental issues and looking for ways to improve the world around us. You see that much of that work requires highly trained career professionals and are wondering whether you also might be able to channel your personal interests into a full-time occupation. You need information on what types of career opportunities there are in environmental fields, what qualifications are required to enter those fields, and how to select the best college to get the training you will need to prepare yourself to pursue your goals and dreams.

If this is your situation, *Education for the Earth* can help you by providing career advice from five of the nation's most prominent environmental leaders and information on over 100 leading undergraduate environmental programs at colleges and universities all across the United States.

CareerWatch 2000

Each of the five authors of the essays in the CareerWatch 2000 section provides his own unique perspective on specific environmental career opportunities, job-related trends, and the type of training needed for jobs in his particular field of endeavor. But when taken together, these essays also provide a great perspective on how government, industry, private nonprofit organizations, and educational institutions are working hand in hand toward the common goal of attaining an environmentally sound world.

The Program Selection Process

The programs presented in this book are the result of research that included initial inquiries at over 600 colleges and universities and information gathered on over 400 programs submitted to us for evaluation. Stringent criteria for inclusion in the book were developed by an advisory board handpicked from the membership of the Alliance for Environmental Education and applied to the submitted programs. The criteria include the following:

(1) The program must be a baccalaureate degree program.

(2) The program must have been in operation for at least four years, i.e., since the fall of 1988.

(3) The program must have a minimum of 30 undergraduate students enrolled, including both majors and minors. (We made a few exceptions to this criterion when we thought the program was particularly noteworthy.)

(4) More than half of the students completing the program must have found a job in their field or gone on to graduate school within six months of graduation.

Among the programs that met these basic criteria, we sought further evidence of a solid, productively managed program, such as:

- being directed by a full or tenured professor;
- sponsoring formal internships or field study opportunities;
- actively promoting interaction between business and government representatives and students through regular programs such as a speakers' series, nonacademic mentoring, and professional forums and conferences;
- supporting regular faculty meetings with business and government advisers to ensure that the course curriculum is preparing students to meet career demands; and
- playing an active role in job placement or sponsoring regularly scheduled career workshops.

The resulting list of published programs is impressive not only in terms of the distinctive approach to environmental education each program offers but also in terms of the breadth and scope of opportunities from which to choose. From planning environmentally effective inner-city landscapes to managing mountainous wilderness, from discovering solutions to toxic waste problems to developing better forest products, from saving the whales to preserving the ozone layer—these are the programs that are training the current generation to make a better world for the next.

The Program Profiles

The program profiles are grouped into five chapters, one for each of five major career fields: Environmental Engineering and Design, Environmental Health, Environmental Science, Environmental Studies, and Natural Resources Management. Within each chapter, the profiles are in alphabetical order by school name.

Note that some careers can be pursued from several different avenues, and thus the categories overlap a little. When this was the case, we tried to pick the category that each program matched best in terms of its overall mission. In particular, at smaller colleges that provide either an environmental studies program or an environmental science program, but not both, the nomenclature often seems interchangeable. We suggest you read David V. McCalley's CareerWatch 2000 essay on environmental education for a discussion of these two types of programs, then check both profile chapters if these are your interests.

Each profile provides basic information on the specific program and the institution that supports it; the mission of the program; the majors and concentrations in which students may enroll; campus facilities, internships, field study, cooperative work-study programs, and other special learning opportunities for students; the typical pursuits of graduates, both career paths chosen and advanced study pursued; and on-campus recruitment efforts. Familiarizing yourself with the format of the profiles will help you review them and compare schools easily.

Indexes and Resources

Since many of the profiles contain technical and esoteric language, we've provided a brief glossary of environmental terminology in the back of the book. In addition, since we know that a book like ours can really only be a starting point for determining your plans, we've provided a reading and resource list that contains a wide variety of information sources about professional environmentalists and environmental career choices.

Finally, we've provided an alphabetical index of the colleges and universities that allows you to look up particular schools in which you are interested and find out what programs they offer, as well as a geographical index that permits you to look up programs in a particular state.

Fast Facts About the Program Lists enrollment and faculty figures, number of degrees conferred, and who to contact.

Fast Facts About the School Lists enrollment and faculty figures, full-time state resident and nonresident tuition, and who to contact.

Major(s)/ Concentration(s) Shows at a glance the major(s) offered and the concentration(s) available.

Who's Recruiting Who on Campus Provides a listing of employers that have gone to the campus in the last two academic years and the positions they were seeking to fill.

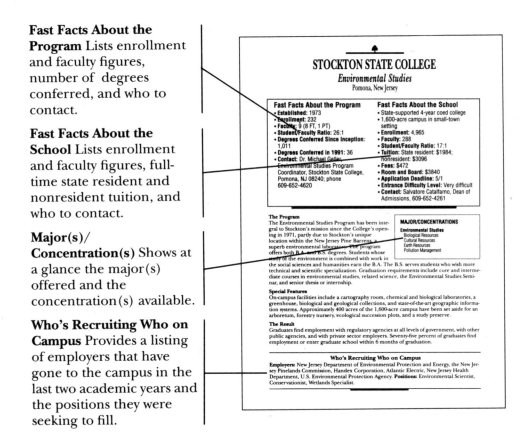

STOCKTON STATE COLLEGE
Environmental Studies
Pomona, New Jersey

Fast Facts About the Program
- **Established:** 1973
- **Enrollment:** 232
- **Faculty:** 9 (8 FT, 1 PT)
- **Student/Faculty Ratio:** 26:1
- **Degrees Conferred Since Inception:** 1,011
- **Degrees Conferred in 1991:** 36
- **Contact:** Dr. Michael Geller, Environmental Studies Program Coordinator, Stockton State College, Pomona, NJ 08240; phone 609-652-4620

Fast Facts About the School
- State-supported 4-year coed college
- 1,600-acre campus in small-town setting
- **Enrollment:** 4,965
- **Faculty:** 288
- **Student/Faculty Ratio:** 17:1
- **Tuition:** State resident: $1984; nonresident: $3096
- **Fees:** $472
- **Room and Board:** $3840
- **Application Deadline:** 5/1
- **Entrance Difficulty Level:** Very difficult
- **Contact:** Salvatore Catalfamo, Dean of Admissions, 609-652-4261

The Program
The Environmental Studies Program has been integral to Stockton's mission since the College's opening in 1971, partly due to Stockton's unique location within the New Jersey Pine Barrens, a superb environmental laboratory. The program offers both B.A. and B.S. degrees. Students whose study of the environment is combined with work in the social sciences and humanities earn the B.A. The B.S. serves students who wish more technical and scientific specialization. Graduation requirements include core and intermediate courses in environmental studies, related science, the Environmental Studies Seminar, and senior thesis or internship.

MAJOR/CONCENTRATIONS
Environmental Studies
Biological Resources
Cultural Resources
Earth Resources
Pollution Management

Special Features
On-campus facilities include a cartography room, chemical and biological laboratories, a greenhouse, biological and geological collections, and state-of-the-art geographic information systems. Approximately 400 acres of the 1,600-acre campus have been set aside for an arboretum, forestry nursery, ecological succession plots, and a study preserve.

The Result
Graduates find employment with regulatory agencies at all levels of government, with other public agencies, and with private sector employers. Seventy-five percent of graduates find employment or enter graduate school within 6 months of graduation.

Who's Recruiting Who on Campus
Employers: New Jersey Department of Environmental Protection and Energy, the New Jersey Pinelands Commission, Handex Corporation, Atlantic Electric, New Jersey Health Department, U.S. Environmental Protection Agency. **Positions:** Environmental Scientist, Conservationist, Wetlands Specialist.

CareerWatch
2000

CareerWatch 2000

A Basic Primer

Steven C. Kussmann

I f you've picked up this book, chances are you are interested in the environment and perhaps may be considering a professional environmental career. If that's the case, this guide is designed for you. First, it will help you learn where the environmental job opportunities are for the next two decades. And second, it will introduce you to some of the leading undergraduate degree programs that are available at over 100 colleges and universities throughout the United States.

Why an Environmental Career?

The environment is important to all of us. Overpopulation, depletion of the ozone layer, water shortages, deforestation, and extinction are all frightening conditions we all face. Our awareness of these problems is growing, and we know that each one of us can make a difference in protecting the environment by recognizing that what we do has an effect. In fact, real progress toward solving the world's environmental problems depends on you. Everything we do has an effect on the environment. We know that in order to rescue our planet we need more information. We need the knowledge to begin forming solutions. So we use less water, carpool or ride a bicycle whenever we can, and recycle. We take the time to examine how we are living and what we are buying.

What Are the Hottest Fields?

If your own commitment goes beyond these measures and you're thinking of becoming a professional environmentalist, there are many types of jobs that are available today. Furthermore, there is no doubt our global ecological

THE MAKING OF AN AWARD-WINNING YOUNG ENVIRONMENTALIST

Profile: Bianca Perla
Graduating Senior
Bellarmine Preparatory School
Tacoma, Washington

Biggest Influences: Bianca has participated in Bellarmine's marine science program under the direction of a dedicated and innovative teacher for the past four years. As part of this program, she has had numerous outstanding opportunities for hands-on experience in environmental science. For example, summer field study trips took her to Hood Canal and to the San Juan Islands in Washington state, where she and her classmates each earned their scuba diving license, and to the Hawaii Institute of Marine Biology at Coconut Island. She attended Bellarmine's summer school and night school science programs every year, taking workshops in scientific notation, statistics, computer graphics, data collection, scientific instrumentation, and research methodologies.

"Living in Tacoma, we're faced with an industrial wasteland where 100 percent of the wetlands have been destroyed. We can see the daily effects of industry and what we are really doing to the earth. Just seeing that day after day gets people motivated to go out there and do something to change it."

She and her classmates entered a project in the Seiko Youth Challenge, a nationwide high school competition in which high school students are invited to identify, research, analyze, and propose a solution to a local environmental problem. The team—which ultimately became a national finalist—proposed a plan to develop a portion of Puget Sound's devastated wetlands into a marine sanctuary, a plan that is now being implemented.

Future Career Plans: To teach at the college level or go into field research in marine biology.

Lifetime Goals: To determine why the world's oceans and coral reefs are being destroyed and to make the world aware of what's wrong and how to fix it.

situation promises that the number of job opportunities in environmentally related fields will increase over the next decade. Several areas such as water quality protection, environmental risk analysis, and environmental design are relatively new. But pressing issues in more established fields are also creating new jobs. A proliferation of environmental mandates has created more jobs in government regulation at the federal, regional, state, and local levels. Technology has created jobs in research, engineering, management, and public interest.

Advances in energy efficiency and the use of renewable energy have created jobs for environmental protection engineers. Technical advances also have created the need for skilled mechanical engineers, applications programmers, and environmental scientists. Research in renewable energy technologies is leading to new trends in improved energy efficiency. More research is also needed.

In the health field, the number of job opportunities remains high. Environmental pollutants have created health problems that will exist for years to come. Hazardous chemicals carried in air and water are entering the workplace and the home, posing short- and long-term threats to human health.

Oceans cover more than two thirds of the earth's surface and are delicately balanced ecosystems. Protecting our oceans is of fundamental importance. Recent progress in protecting marine resources includes improved management of ocean fisheries and a number of international and regional initiatives to control pollution. Marine science is an important new field in environmental professions. You will find several excellent undergraduate programs in marine science profiled in this book.

Environmental educators are benefiting from training and workshops offered through centers for environmental education in every state. Colleges and universities offer teacher training, as do state nonprofit organizations dedicated to the protection of wildlife and habitats. Environmental education is now mandated for school-aged children in many states. Millions of children benefit from nature walks and classroom demonstrations. Science projects give teachers and students hands-on science experience through nature. Teacher training and public education programs are the key to helping people make intelligent choices in protecting the environment. An important part of schoolchildren's academic training is providing them with programs that excite them about the delicate world around them. Environmental educators are needed, too, to build an understanding of public policy that supports a sustainable environment for generations to come.

What Schooling and Skills Are Needed?

Tomorrow's professional environmentalist will require formal education and many different abilities and interests. The technical skills required for many of these jobs—in chemistry, biology, engineering, systems analysis, mathematics, computer science, environmental studies, law, management, accounting, communications, and many other areas—will require college or university training. Browse through the programs offered at the universities and colleges listed in this guide—they are among the best in the nation—to get a feel for the courses of study that will take you where you want to go.

THE MAKING OF AN AWARD-WINNING YOUNG ENVIRONMENTALIST

Profile: Wendi Shelor
Graduating Senior
Pinewood Preparatory School
Summerville, South Carolina

Biggest Influences: Wendi has participated in Pinewood's environmental science program for the past three years. The curriculum is based on a college-level environmental biology textbook. As an example of the many opportunities provided by this class, she and her classmates attended seminars on the water cycle of their local area and then came back and made a presentation to the third and fourth graders at their school on what they had learned.

At the suggestion of her environmental science teacher, she attended a one-week environmental camp each summer to learn about conservation and wildlife preservation. "That's what really got me started in my environmental interests."

The high school students at Pinewood are responsible for carrying out Earth Day as a consciousness-raising event each year to educate the younger students about environmental issues. The older students prepare the grounds and form the gardens over spring break, then on Earth Day every student plants a tree or a plant to beautify the school, the older students helping and teaching the little ones.

Wendi and her classmates entered a project in the Seiko Youth Challenge, a nationwide high school competition in which high school students are invited to identify, research, analyze, and propose a solution to a local environmental problem. The team—which ultimately became the national award winner—proposed a countywide plan to locate and remove hundreds of potentially leaky underground gasoline storage tanks from defunct and now forgotten service stations and other unregistered sites.

Future Career Plans: To become an environmental lawyer.

Life Goals and Ambitions: To bring about an overall cultural change that makes being fully environmentally conscious the norm and ensures the passing of environmentally sound practices from one generation to the next at every level of living.

Where Do You Start?

If you are interested in exploring environmental careers, begin now. Educate yourself. Education helps to raise awareness. And knowing is half the battle. Subscribe to publications that can tell you about current programs. Seek summer jobs that are related to environmental protection—state and local park programs are a good place to start.

Read books on sustainable development to find out how to become active in your community on environmental, energy, and related issues. Join environmental organizations—promoting information-sharing in your community will help you to know that what you do can make a difference. Visit a college or university near you. Talk with others already in the field. And of course, explore the environmental studies programs listed in this book.

The Challenge Is Rewarding

To solve the environmental problems we are facing in years to come, we need more future-oriented thinkers, more information, and improved practices. You can make a difference by entering into a challenging environmental career that helps other people, the community, and the world. If you're about to make a decision about where to go to college, this book can help in identifying environmental career opportunities and some exciting environmentally related education paths.

———————— ♠ ————————

Steven C. Kussmann is director of communications programs at the American Gas Association. He also serves as the Chairman of the Alliance for Environmental Education, a private, nonprofit association of over 240 business, labor, health, educational, and environmental organizations.

CareerWatch 2000

Environmental Education and Careers in Teaching

David V. McCalley

To be an effective advocate for the environment, you sure have to know a lot!" These were the words of one of my students as she reflected on a case study we were doing in class. She went on to relate how valuable her general studies courses were in providing her with a clearer picture of the case study. Her major was economics, and our case study had to do with imagining a sustainable world future. She found her course work in economics alone was not enough to provide her with the vision she needed. She felt she had greater success in developing that vision when she also called on what she had learned in her general studies courses.

This is the essence of environmental studies. No one academic discipline can provide all of the information and insight needed for coping with problems related to our environment. This may be the first great lesson to learn when confronting environmental issues.

Environmental Studies vs. Environmental Science

You probably have heard people talk about environmental studies and environmental science. While it is true that the two terms are often used interchangeably, the actual fields of study are different but related. Environmental studies is a broad field in which environmental issues are examined using applications from life and physical sciences, social sciences, and humanities (art, literature, philosophy, etc.). Environmental science is a much narrower field. Its focus is on providing a scientific basis for analyzing environmental problems. A quick way to distinguish between the two is to recognize that environmental studies involves politics—the thoughts and biases of a variety of people—and environmental science involves scientific analysis. The great hope and expectation of most people concerned about the environment is that the politics of environmental issues will direct attention to the science of environmental problems.

As you look through the many listings in this book, you will find that some colleges and universities emphasize environmental studies and others emphasize environmental science. Others provide a hybrid program in which a science discipline may become the student's major field of study and environmental studies may become a minor field.

The College Entrance Examination Board recently surveyed 2,900 colleges and universities and found that 317 of these institutions currently offer majors in environmental science. Other groups have estimated that between 125 and 200 institutions offer majors in environmental studies. The difference in these numbers may be related to the definitions stated above. For example, the College Entrance Examination Board's results included only those institutions listing a major in environmental science. Majors in conservation, fisheries biology, forestry, natural resources, and wildlife biology were not included. In any case, it appears that only about 10 percent of the colleges and universities in the United States are addressing the environment by offering formalized majors.

When looking at courses of study, at one end of the spectrum you'll find majors that focus on special environmental courses, and at the other end you'll find traditional majors (such as biology or geology). Most programs offer either a research or an intern experience for students after their junior year. What follows are two examples of academic majors that focus on the environment.

Environmental Studies. This example illustrates the typical structure of an environmental studies program. Its core courses join science, social science, and the humanities together in the study of specific environmental concerns. Seminars play an important role in this kind of program and give students the opportunity to study and discuss current topics of environmental concern.

The common course requirements of this program include:
- decision making
- environmental systems
- environment
- human ecology
- environmental ethics seminars

Students complete a science core of eight courses in addition to required courses and may choose electives to emphasize a particular area. Electives include aquatic chemistry, conservation biology, environmental nutrition, environmental or behavioral toxicology, groundwater studies, marine or terrestrial ecology, science policy studies, water quality, and watershed studies.

Courses in the science core require three quarters of general biology, three quarters of general chemistry, a course in organic chemistry, and a course in calculus.

A senior thesis or internship is required. The thesis is based on an independent study project designed by the student with faculty advice. It focuses ideas, energy, experience, and training on an environmental issue. In lieu of a thesis, a student may elect to undertake an internship in government, business, or industry. The thesis or internship is normally completed in the senior year and is guided by one or more faculty advisers.

Environmental Science. This example illustrates the typical structure of an environmental science program. It achieves its environmental focus by providing students with environmental courses to be taken in association with an existing science major.

Students must make special application for admission to the environmental science program. Applications are processed by the Environmental Science Advisory Committee. Admission to the program may be granted when the following conditions are met:

1. The student completes the core requirements of his or her chosen Bachelor of Arts science program. Application for admission to the Environmental Science Program usually takes place no later than the semester in which the core requirements are completed.
2. The student completes the introductory course entitled Introduction to Environmental Science.
3. To continue on the Environmental Science track, the student must maintain a minimum grade point average of 2.5 on a scale of 4.0 in the core work and the Introduction to Environmental Science course.

The Environmental Science Program is built on a base of scientific competence equivalent to an undergraduate Bachelor of Arts degree in a science department. This is followed by two semesters of concentration in environmental study constituting what is known as an Environmental Senior Year.

The Basic Science course of study includes:

- completion of the requirements of one of the following undergraduate science majors: biology, chemistry, earth science, geology, or physics
- completion of Introduction to Environmental Science

The Environmental Senior Year course of study includes:

- completion of the Environmental Science Program—3 hours of Environmental Science and 3 hours of electives chosen from the following: applied instrumental analysis, ecology, ecotoxology, environmental applications of physics, environmental chemistry; geochemistry; hydrogeology, and limnology.
- undergraduate research or environmental field experience

You may be wondering which program is best. Neither one is best in an absolute sense. You will find professionals who would champion either of these models or even a model that combines both. Determining which is best for you requires some thought about your life's goals. Seek the views of others whom you can trust to provide you with helpful advice. Most important, examine the criteria for entrance into your chosen profession.

Preparing to Become an Environmental Teacher

The preparation needed to become an environmental educator varies according to the level at which you will be teaching. Typically, to become a certified teacher in an elementary, middle, junior high, or senior high school, you must have at least a bachelor's degree and meet specific state requirements. Teaching at a college level generally requires an advanced degree—M.A., M.S., or Ph.D.

Elementary- and Secondary-Level Teacher Preparation. There is no traditional grammar or secondary school subject that focuses on the environment. In addition, relatively few school districts offer a specific environmental course. However, many states mandate teaching about the environment, and, while it is often integrated into all academic subject areas, occasionally it is only included in the sciences. When teaching about the environment is mandated, it is commonly done for all grade levels. Teachers who recognize the need for environmental education often infuse study about the environment into traditional course offerings. Many environmental educators feel that this is the best way to teach about environmental issues.

Relatively few colleges or universities provide special environmental education courses for preservice teachers. Teachers may attend academic workshops or other programs in order to learn more about the environment and how to teach about it. In the future, more will be expected from all K-12 teachers in the area of environmental education. And it is likely that more colleges and universities will include environmental education in their teacher education curricula.

Internationally, a global perspective on environment education is developing. Many countries are incorporating environmental education into their school curricula. We can look forward to an increasing number of international teacher and student exchanges at the high school level, which can lead to a greater appreciation of the global nature of environmental problems.

College-Level Teacher Preparation. If you're interested in teaching at a two-year community college or technical school, it's likely you'll need to have earned a master's or doctoral degree. Since teaching and not research is the primary responsibility of a community college or technical school instructor, a research degree may prove to be of limited value.

If you're interested in teaching at a four-year institution, while it is essential that you obtain a doctoral degree, there are a variety of paths you can take. The traditional academic areas to major in are biology, chemistry, earth science, and physics. In addition, a number of specialized fields of study exist, including fish and wildlife biology, forestry, natural resources, and soils. Each of these may be divided further into more specific study areas. The highest degree is a doctoral degree—Ph.D or Ed.D.—which requires the student to pose a sound research question, design a study in order to search for answers, and write a dissertation about the process and its outcome.

While the tendency is to become more specialized with each degree, there are those who argue that the environmental scientist needs to be a generalist, capable of integrating data from various sciences while attempting to analyze problems of the environment. Certainly, an environmental scientist must have broad knowledge of social sciences and the humanities. Since environmental issues are resolved through some form of political action, it is important that an environmental scientist be capable of effectively communicating data and the results of scientific inquiry. In the final analysis, the environmental-scientist-in-training must take the general studies portion of a university education as seriously as the scientific portion.

It's been over twenty years since the first Earth Day, and the environment has at long last become an issue of national and global concern. The 1992 Earth Summit, organized by the United Nations Council on Economic Development, affirmed the concern of the nations of the world for the entire biosphere and for human survival. Dedicated students choosing any career that requires the study of the environment as academic or technical background are assured of having an exciting life.

David V. McCalley is professor of biology and science education at the University of Northern Iowa. He is also director of the UNI Institute for Environmental Education.

CareerWatch 2000

Environmental Careers in Government

Robert L. Herbst

The opportunities in government at the local, state, and national levels for conservation and environmental careers are many and diverse. Conservation is growing in importance and in public understanding. There is no question that proper management and protection of our land, water, air, and living resources are essential to our way of life and to the quality of life.

If you are interested in the out-of-doors or you are concerned about the quality of our environment, a satisfying career can be found in a conservation profession. Because of the country's vast public lands, government agencies have been and will continue to be one of the nation's largest employers in the field. These agencies manage the lands, which include national and state parks, and have authority in zoning, research, regulation, recreation, mapping, and other activities.

There is no single, typical conservation job for you to consider. On the contrary, the opportunities are varied. In addition, some of tomorrow's environmental careers have not been invented yet. Whatever you ultimately choose to pursue will require hard work and deep commitment. Now is the time to think through your own interests and unique skills—going through the process will help you with your goal. Special courses that relate to the profession you are considering or summer jobs that give you a taste of an employment area are great ways to start. Write or visit the schools listed in this directory that appeal to you. They will be delighted to fill your mailbox with information on courses and requirements.

Keep in mind that the best preparation for an environmental career is a basic education. Remember, too, that as important as what you know is what you can do. Develop skills beyond what you learn in school by volunteering in your community and taking on part-time jobs. Furthermore, know that every environmental field is constantly changing. New problems, research, and technology require keeping current. You must be willing to adapt.

Let's look at a few specific professions.

Forestry. In our nation, one third of the land is covered with forests—and there are trees in our yards, our parks, and along our boulevards as well. Trees individually and collectively have many benefits—timber and paper products, for starters. They also cleanse the air and hold the soil. Forests are home to wildlife and fish. They provide outdoor recreation and in the West, for example, grazing land for sheep and cattle.

The forester's job is challenging and complex, involving managing not only trees but all biological organisms of the forest for products and enjoyment. Forestry also requires the ability to work with people, and many foresters must have administrative and business skills.

A career in forestry generally requires a college degree from a school offering professional training in the field. There are, in addition, technical disciplines related to forest management that also require degrees. These require special training for the specific skill.

What are the employment opportunities for foresters in government? There are many. The U.S. Forest Service employs thousands of professionals in national parks. Other federal land areas requiring foresters are administered by the Tennessee Valley Authority, the Bureau of Land Management, and even the Department of Defense. Still other forests and public lands are administered by states, counties, or municipalities. Usually, government employment requires an applicant to pass an entrance exam.

Good sources for information on these opportunities and on how to apply to specific agencies are available from your college career counselor and the personnel office of the agency you are interested in. You can also contact the Society of American Foresters, 5400 Grosvenor Lane, Bethesda, Maryland 20814-7198.

Parks and Outdoor Recreation. People love the out-of-doors. Over 60 million Americans fish. Camping, boating, hunting, bird watching, skiing, and hiking are just some of the other activities millions of Americans enjoy outdoors.

Jobs in this growing field require people who have an understanding of nature and history. Protection of resources, traditional values, planning and designing facilities, and administering recreational services are important facets of the field.

Educational requirements for recreation careers are as diverse as the types of careers available. Professionals include park rangers, park historians, archeologists, foresters, and naturalists. Keep in mind that such jobs require understanding in many academic subject areas, including basic sciences, communications, earth sciences, mathematics, administration, and biological sciences.

Employment opportunities in this area are far ranging, but the pay is low. Every city and state has a park, as do the National Park Service, the U.S. Forest Service, the Tennessee Valley Authority, the Bureau of Land Management, and many other federal agencies. These organizations may also have programs in outdoor recreation.

Career counseling and seeking out opportunities on your own are great ways to start your job search. Visit your local library for books such as *The Conservation Directory* and *The Complete Guide to Finding Jobs in Government.* Or, while you are still in high school, contact your local park authority and talk to the superintendent about volunteer opportunities in conservation programs.

Soil Conservation. Soil produces crops, it is the foundation of buildings, and it sustains pasture lands. Soil conservationists can be found in many professions, and the jobs involving soil conservation are varied. Typical responsibilities involve assessing soil, protecting it from erosion, and implementing practices that increase productivity. Other jobs include mapping and the design of dams for flood protection.

In this field, a farming or ranching background is highly desirable, as are college-level study and training in soil science, soil conservation, range conservation, agriculture, and economics, to name a few. However, while the majority of positions relating to soil conservation require college degrees, a number do not. These supervised positions generally require technical training.

Most jobs in this field are in the government sector. The U.S. Department of Agriculture (USDA), particularly its Soil Conservation Service, is a principal employer and can be an excellent source of information on this career field. Soil conservationists and related professionals and technical workers are very much in demand by the TVA, the Department of the Interior, and many state and local units of federal agencies.

County agents and those who work for the extension service of the USDA are good contacts to make when seeking information on the profession.

Watershed Management. Water covers three fourths of the earth's surface. It is life itself—life for the tiniest microorganisms, the great whales, and human beings. Water is everyone's business and everyone's interest. Watershed management is a growing field and can result in increased water supplies and improved water quality, erosion control, and flood prevention.

Watershed includes not just a body of water, river, or stream but also the land adjacent to it. Pollution control, hydrologic studies, global warming assessments on water levels, ocean dumping, and regulating reservoir yields are just a few of the kinds of jobs that exist in this field.

Jobs in watershed management generally require a college degree. If you attend an institution that offers a watershed management curriculum, it's a good idea to take advantage of course offerings in related fields, including hydrology, geology, and range management.

Employment can be found in state and local conservation and pollution control agencies and in cities needing experts in waste management and in providing drinking water. The Environmental Protection Agency, U.S. Forest Service, and many other federal agencies will continue to provide employment opportunities.

Progress and change in today's world have brought with them a series of new problems and needs to be addressed by conservation professionals and supporting technicians. But in addition to committed people to work in this important and growing field is the need to educate the general population about the environment. In the long run it is the use of resources—people's habits and attitudes and a nation's needs—that dictate environmental policies and economic progress. Increasing the level of understanding about the world around us is essential to our ultimate environmental health.

✦

Robert L. Herbst is the Washington representative for the Tennessee Valley Authority. He was formerly president of the Lake Superior Center for Freshwater Understanding and executive director of Trout Unlimited.

CareerWatch 2000

Environmental Careers in the Corporate World

Kenneth T. Derr

The 1990s are shaping up to be the "Decade of the Environment." There's a greater awareness of the impact we are having on the environment, and there's a growing corporate commitment to a higher environmental ethic. It's also clear that environmental and economic issues are closely interwoven into the very fabric of our society. Virtually everyone wants both a healthier environment and a better quality of life for future generations. As a result, I'd encourage young Americans who want to be a part of this drive for a better tomorrow to consider technically oriented careers that improve the quality of our air, land, water, and wildlife. While rapid growth in the environmental field began in the 1980s, there is still plenty of opportunity ahead.

I think the greatest activities on the environmental front likely will take place in the corporate sector. Industry is faced with enormous challenges to clean up past practices and to operate in more environmentally benign ways in the future. Industry also can make the biggest contribution to environmental betterment because it has the financial resources, the experience, the technical know-how, and the incentive. It's clear that the times have truly changed in this field. In the past, a corporate environmental career may have been viewed by some as a dead end. After the first Earth Day in 1970, industrial America often was cast as the environmental villain because of its past practices. And when regulations were passed in the late 1970s, much of industry questioned the changes and feared the costs. Today, however, we're entering a new era of corporate environmentalism. Some are calling this the "eco-industrial revolution" or the "greening of American business."

This corporate environmental movement is happening for two main reasons. First, business realizes that safeguarding the environment is the ethical thing to do. Second, companies that fail to demonstrate high environmental principles will not survive the 1990s. They will either be shut down by government regulation, or their customers will find a more enlightened competitor elsewhere. In many ways, the petrochemical industry is a leader in this new wave of corporate environmentalism. Our industry was the first major sector of the economy that faced tight environmental regulations. As a result, petrochemical companies are more advanced than many other industries in cleanup and pollution-prevention technology and in the expertise of their environmental work force.

The need for environmental skills in business has spread rapidly. As regulations have become more complex and costly, the need for health-and-safety specialists has quickly branched out into environmental affairs. What were once basic compliance programs have evolved into strategic programs developed to avoid the costs associated with pollution. As a result, there's been a growing demand in industry for professionals and others with specialized training in air, land, water, and wildlife protection, management and regulatory and legal processes.

In recent years, industry has evolved into an era of not just complying with stricter regulations but also anticipating them by voluntarily finding new and less harmful ways to operate. Those industries that solve technical environmental problems before regulations are proposed will be the most successful. That's why we're on the lookout for people with innovative approaches. For example, in the petrochemical industry, we're developing cleaner conventional transportation fuels. We're designing new ways to reduce or eliminate pollutants that go into the air, land, and water. And we're developing practical alternative fuels, such as compressed natural gas, to power vehicles.

Undoubtedly, the largest regulatory impact on industry in recent years has been the passage of the Clean Air Act Amendments of 1990. For example, in our industry, major investments and innovations to meet the new regulations will require modifications in refineries making new fuels, in facilities making new gasoline-blending components, in blending and storage units at refineries, and at gas stations and other sales outlets. It's estimated that the cost to comply with the Clean Air Act Amendments for the petroleum industry alone will range annually from $15 billion to $23 billion. Although the costs are great, the opportunities for creative and efficient solutions are even greater. This is an area where future environmental talent will be in great demand.

Environmentally related careers can take many paths, ranging from biology and industrial hygiene to legal and regulatory matters. However, industry's greatest need will be for people schooled in the core sciences, such as engineering and chemistry, whose skills can be adapted to a company's specific environmental problems. Graduates with hard-science disciplines who can adjust to a variety of new responsibilities will have a competitive advantage. Typically, more than 40 percent of the new professionals Chevron hires are recent engineering graduates.

As in all technical jobs, the corporate world is looking for environmental specialists who have demonstrated exceptional academic ability in college.

But we also recognize that job applicants don't just need to have a body of technical knowledge. They must develop a disciplined way of thinking that can be applied to a wide range of business activities and opportunities. You'll find that learning generally continues—and sometimes intensifies—after you receive your college diploma. Education is a lifelong process, and at most companies there's a lot more training after you have your diploma in your hand. We've found that those who learn well in school also tend to learn well on the job.

We're also looking for a lot more than just academic excellence. We want well-rounded people who possess leadership qualities, a sense of commitment to their community, an understanding of the value of teamwork, and a mature attitude and understanding regarding their careers. In addition, a fair number of new hires have already held jobs with progressive responsibilities while they were in school. This shows us they can do well in the practical side of life.

It's also crucial that job aspirants possess a good ability to communicate one-on-one and in group settings. Interpersonal skills are especially important for nearly everyone involved in the environmental arena. Much of the corporate environmentalist's job is to digest, analyze, and relate complex information about problems and solutions both inside and outside the company and act as a liaison among differing groups.

Once on board, an employee may work in a rural refinery as a safety coordinator or in an urban skyscraper interpreting legislative proposals. He or she may be testing wastewater for traces of contaminants or monitoring marine life near an offshore drilling platform. This "corporate environmentalist" may be checking crude oil loading procedures on a supertanker or designing "scrubbers" that reduce air emissions in a chemical plant.

I should also mention another significant trend in the corporate work force of the future: more and more opportunities are moving overseas where business prospects are the greatest. For example, at Chevron, we've recently relied on a variety of environmental disciplines to make sure oil-drilling operations deep in the rain forests of Papua New Guinea don't harm the surrounding plant and animal life and to protect the frozen tundra in the arctic regions of Alaska's North Slope.

Because the scope of corporate environmental issues is so large, the opportunities are also tremendous. This is particularly true in large international companies. Take Chevron, for example. Chevron is the fourth-largest petroleum company in the United States and the sixth-largest in the world. We are the largest refiner and marketer of petroleum products in the United States and the largest U.S. producer of natural gas. We are the working home of about 50,000 people who are based in over 100 countries. Chevron currently has about 550 full-time employees who specialize in environmental matters, working in jobs that demand a wide variety of backgrounds. About two thirds come from the chemical, mechanical, and civil engineering disciplines. Chemical and geology backgrounds form the next group and include about 12 percent of our formal environmental work force. The rest come from toxicology, microbiology, and other science backgrounds, and there are also those with legal and business training.

However, putting a precise number value on the total magnitude and range of the corporate environmental work force is virtually impossible. That's because many people beyond those in jobs dedicated to environmental responsibilities spend a significant portion of their time on environmental work. For example, by the very nature of the petrochemical industry and its related land, coal, and mineral operations, environmental concerns have become incorporated in one way or another into literally thousands of jobs. Refinery and chemical operators, attorneys, mining company employees, government affairs representatives, office assistants, finance and personnel specialists must deal with environmental issues everyday, and most professional employees take classes to sensitize them to environmental issues, whether they work in human resources, tax, or public affairs.

If we as a nation and world believe every job must have some stake in protecting the environment, then we must ensure that environmental concerns are integrated into all major business decisions. For example, the international Business Council for Sustainable Development, of which I am a member, helped influence discussion at the Earth Summit in Rio de Janeiro. One of the council's overriding conclusions is that the world community must find reasonable solutions that balance environmental protection with economic development. How to achieve and sustain this balance will be an increasingly critical issue for tomorrow's environmental problem solvers.

These are the kinds of issues corporate America is wrestling with these days. Most forward-thinking companies want to be recognized as leaders in environment, health, and safety performance, to be a part of the solution to environmental problems, and to manage risk so that they can reduce liabilities and gain competitive advantage. The only way to do that is to hire bright, creative, and motivated people who can do the job right. It's not an easy job. The environmental issues and problems in the corporate arena are complex, and they're often very frustrating. But the potential rewards are also enormous. A price tag can't be put on the satisfaction of knowing you've helped make the world a healthier place.

I wish you much good fortune in choosing a career and hope these thoughts have helped you in that very important pursuit.

Kenneth T. Derr is chairman of the board and chief executive officer of Chevron Corporation. He is also a director of Citicorp and the American Petroleum Institute.

CareerWatch 2000

Environmental Careers in the Nonprofit Sector

Jay D. Hair

In 1988, the National Wildlife Federation received eighty applications for twelve openings for interns at its headquarters in Washington, D.C. In 1992, the total number of applicants rose to 350. These numbers illustrate a dilemma for nonprofit conservation organizations: there is rapidly growing interest in working to save the environment, but most nonprofits do not have the financial resources to hire as many people as are needed.

There is no question that concern about the environment is strong. An NWF poll of undergraduates across the nation showed that 95 percent of students believe that Congress should pass tougher laws to protect the environment. Ninety-four percent said that students can make a difference in environmental protection, and the same number were willing to pay more for products that are environmentally safe.

A recent Gallup Poll indicated that 11 percent of Americans are active in an environmental group. Estimates of the number of people belonging to one or more conservation organizations in the United States range from about 10 to 40 million. The Federation has grown in recent years to include 5.3 million members, and many other groups have also enjoyed relatively steady increases.

The number of nonprofit conservation groups also has grown. The total in 1992 was estimated by knowledgeable professionals at about 5,000, including national organizations as well as regional, state, and local groups. Some of the larger groups have memberships in the millions, while smaller local groups sometimes bring together only a few people.

Some of those organizations have sizable staffs. The Federation employs about 600 at its Washington headquarters and its Conservation Education Center in Vienna, Virginia, plus thirty-five others at its regional offices around the country. On the other end of the spectrum are smaller groups that have no paid staffs and operate through the services of a few volunteers.

Because the size of such operations often changes, it is difficult to specify exact employment numbers nationwide. But some experts estimate that there are about 10,000 professional positions among all U.S. nonprofit conservation groups and an additional 5,000 or so support jobs.

The number of positions opening up each year across the nation is estimated to total about 1,000—thus accounting for the keen competition among college graduates, professionals changing jobs within the field, and additional qualified candidates from other walks of life. In addition, layoffs in both the public and private sectors in recent years have contributed to the relative abundance of candidates for openings in the early 1990s.

Nevertheless, most nonprofit groups—including the Federation—are looking for promising newcomers to the field. It takes no crystal ball to realize that the future of conservation depends on young people who are now in college or who are about to enter undergraduate programs. After all, while young people make up 50 percent of our population today, they represent 100 percent of our future. It is clear that increasing public concern about the environment will result in ever-growing demands for more action to protect it—and more jobs to ensure that those demands are met.

Many colleges and universities now have programs to equip graduates for employment in environmental work in positions ranging from field biologists to waste-materials managers. This is excellent training and should go a long way toward improving future approaches to conserving the environment.

One fast-growing field is environmental health. Qualifications for workers in this area often involve a concentration of study in subjects such as health engineering, health physics, and occupational epidemiology. In addition, demands are increasing for energy conservation specialists.

But there is also a growing need for workers in activities that do not necessarily involve a specialty in science. Because of increasingly complex laws and regulations concerning the environment, more and more people are needed in Washington and the state capitals to carry the concerns of conservationists to Congress and the legislatures. This means lawyers or other articulate people who can act as spokespersons and who have backgrounds in areas such as English literature and history. Dealing with legislative and regulatory affairs will definitely be a growth industry in the coming decades.

At the same time, many conservation groups, including the Federation, are driven by a grass-roots constituency. This requires a well-trained staff for regional services and action. Working with grass-roots constituents to address local and regional concerns will remain a vital part of the national conservation movement and will continue to require well-trained grass-roots coordinators.

People from all sorts of academic fields have also made their marks in nonprofits in work such as administration, fund-raising, and membership promotion. Professionals in many nonprofits say these activities are expanding in their organizations.

A background that includes a range of environmental studies helps to get a job and promotions in most conservation organizations. But there are places for graduates from most disciplines, especially if a candidate shows a general excellence resulting from intelligence, initiative, and dedication.

Most nonprofits need people who communicate well, both as speakers and writers. Consequently, graduates with degrees in English and communications are often considered favorably. As the world's environmental concerns have become more complex with far-reaching human impact, participants in environmental protection have become more diverse. Many nonprofits are actively encouraging African Americans, Hispanics, Native Americans, and others to investigate career possibilities in the field.

Some of the largest conservation organizations have cooperated to establish a Human Environment Center, which acts as a job and resource bank for minorities. One of the center's functions is to send out circulars to schools informing minorities of career opportunities and offering advice on study programs leading to securing those jobs.

After graduation from college, most successful applicants find permanent employment with the nonprofits by serving first as interns—with or without pay. Another avenue is through volunteer work, which is the backbone of many of the smaller groups. Normally, only college graduates are hired for professional jobs, although some support positions are available to applicants with high school diplomas.

Hundreds of internships are available nationwide within the nonprofit conservation sector. These positions provide valuable hands-on experience in areas ranging from resource work to educational programs to campus outreach.

For interns in the Federation's Resources and Conservation Department, typical duties might include helping with a report on clean lakes, doing research on genetically engineered food, or assisting with the presentation of materials on ancient forests to lawmakers on Capitol Hill. Interns with the Research and Education Department help as registrars, instructors, and coordinators at NWF's Camps and Summits® and also assist in developing nature-education materials and programs. Campus Outreach interns work with college students to develop sustainable environmental changes on college campuses across the country.

The NWF, like many of its counterparts, every year sends out circulars to colleges listing internship possibilities. Most applications we get come from these mailings. Many nonprofits also take part in environmental job fairs held in cities across the country. Those fairs bring in lots of inquiries.

Many interns at the Federation have an undergraduate degree in environmental science. Other organizations, especially with extensive field operations, often put a premium on degrees such as biology and botany.

Once on our permanent staff, employees have the opportunity to move far and wide. Pay for clerical positions starts in the teens and moves up from there. Some typical jobs: an assistant magazine editor makes $25,000 a year, a resource specialist is paid $33,000 a year, and the base pay for a vice president is in the $60,000 range, although that may go higher. Some administrative posts pay more than $100,000.

As an example of how the system works, one of our vice presidents, who has a liberal arts degree and a long history of working in environmental affairs, came to Washington as a lobbyist in the early 1970s. Then she was hired by the Federation to work on issues involving Alaska and worked her way up to her present position.

Other large organizations offer comparable opportunities. The Wilderness Society has a pay scale that starts at $16,000 for a secretary or administrative assistant and increases to $95,000 for a vice president.

The National Audubon Society pays $15,000 to clerical assistants. The range of pay for an associate scientist is $26,900 to $44,400 and from $19,800 to $32,700 for an environmental education specialist. At the vice president's level and above, the pay can go as high as $100,000 and more.

So the opportunities are definitely there, even though the competition for jobs can be tough. Some of the best advice for aspiring conservationists is to plan early for your career. As soon as you can, narrow down the choices to something you really want to do; try to pick a specialty, not simply a general area. Often that specialized knowledge and experience will make a difference in your favor when it comes to being hired for that critical first job— and all the promotions that should follow. Another bit of advice: volunteer as much as you can for any and all environmental activities that come your way before graduation. That experience and dedication will count heavily when it comes time to apply for a job.

Jay D. Hair is president and CEO of the National Wildlife Federation. He serves on a number of boards of directors and is chairperson of the board and president of the World Conservation Union and its North American regional councilor.

Environmental Engineering and Design

Environmental engineering and design programs span an array of applied mathematics and science disciplines that train professionals to develop, construct, or modify structures, sites, machines, products, systems, or processes to the benefit of the environment.

LOUISIANA STATE UNIVERSITY AND AGRICULTURAL AND MECHANICAL COLLEGE
Environmental Engineering
Baton Rouge, Louisiana

Fast Facts About the Program
- **Established:** 1978
- **Enrollment:** 150
- **Faculty:** 7 (5 FT, 2 PT)
- **Student/Faculty Ratio:** 21:1
- **Degrees Conferred Since Inception:** 700
- **Degrees Conferred in 1991:** 30
- **Contact:** Dr. Dipak Roy, Department of Civil Engineering, Louisiana State University and Agricultural and Mechanical College, Baton Rouge, LA 70803; phone 504-388-8442

Fast Facts About the School
- State-supported coed university
- 1,944-acre campus in urban setting
- **Enrollment:** 26,138
- **Faculty:** 1,348
- **Student/Faculty Ratio:** 19:1
- **Tuition:** State resident: $2058; nonresident: $5258
- **Room and Board:** $2710
- **Application Deadline:** 7/1
- **Entrance Difficulty Level:** Moderately difficult
- **Contact:** Lisa Harris, Director of Admissions, 504-388-1175

The Program

The Environmental Engineering Program, traditionally part of the Department of Civil Engineering, has an emphasis on water treatment and distribution and collection and disposal of industrial and municipal wastewater. In 1978, the department began developing state-of-the-art environmental teaching and research laboratories. The department instituted a major curriculum revision that greatly expanded course offerings to cover air pollution, modeling of environmental systems, groundwater and surface water management, and hazardous- and solid-waste disposal. Louisiana State University also offers programs in biological and agricultural engineering and in industrial engineering.

MAJOR/CONCENTRATIONS
Civil/Environmental Engineering
Air Quality
Aquaculture and Environmental Modeling
Industrial and Hazardous Waste Management
Management of Natural Ecosystems and Wetlands
Solid Wastes
Water and Wastewater Treatment

Special Features

The Environmental Engineering Program is administered through the Department of Civil Engineering, with support from the Louisiana Water Resources Research Institute, the Louisiana Geological Survey, the Sea Grant Program, the Coastal Zone Management Program, the Remote Sensing and Image Processing Laboratory, the Louisiana Transportation Research Center, and the Hazardous Waste Research Center. The program is a major participant with Texas A&M University and Mississippi State University in the U.S. Army Corps of Engineers Graduate Institute at the Waterways Experiment Station in Vicksburg. Interinstitutional programs are also maintained with Southern University in Baton Rouge.

The Result

Almost all students with an environmental engineering background are recruited by government and the private sector, including chemical and petrochemical industries, waste management industries, engineering consulting firms, and construction companies. Many pursue graduate studies in environmental engineering at LSU and other universities. All graduates find employment or enroll in graduate school within 6 months of graduation.

LOUISIANA STATE UNIVERSITY AND AGRICULTURAL AND MECHANICAL COLLEGE
Landscape Architecture
Baton Rouge, Louisiana

Fast Facts About the Program
- **Established:** 1942
- **Enrollment:** 160
- **Faculty:** 16 (all FT)
- **Student/Faculty Ratio:** 10:1
- **Degrees Conferred Since Inception:** 800
- **Degrees Conferred in 1991:** 40
- **Environmental Library:** Yes
- **Contact:** Bruce Sharky, Director, School of Landscape Architecture, Louisiana State University and Mechanical College, Baton Rouge, LA 70803; phone 504-388-1434

Fast Facts About the School
- State-supported coed university
- 1,944-acre campus in urban setting
- **Enrollment:** 26,138
- **Faculty:** 1,348
- **Student/Faculty Ratio:** 19:1
- **Tuition:** State resident: $2058; nonresident: $5258
- **Room and Board:** $2710
- **Application Deadline:** 7/1
- **Entrance Difficulty Level:** Moderately difficult
- **Contact:** Lisa Harris, Director of Admissions, 504-388-1175

The Program
Undergraduates receive a balanced education in communication, construction, design, and theory. The curriculum includes environmental policy, preservation of historical landscapes, studio work and theory in regional planning, computer technology, and urban design. Assignments often involve community projects. Each year over 25 scholarships are awarded through the Landscape Architecture Foundation.

MAJOR

Landscape Architecture

Special Features
The School owns and operates the Hilltop Arboretum, which specializes in native and selectively introduced species of subtropical southern Louisiana. Cooperative education programs provide students with the opportunity to work with government agencies and private companies. The exchange programs allow students to study in Scotland, Japan, and Italy. The school, together with the College of Design, has an active speaker and guest design critic series. Design Week, a yearly event, brings a renowned design professional to work with teams of graduates and undergraduates in a design competition.

The Result
Landscape architects pursue unique opportunities to improve the quality of life in cities and outdoor surroundings, including the design of parks, recreation facilities, urban public spaces, business parks, private gardens, zoos, and regional and rural landscapes.

Who's Recruiting Who on Campus
Employers (Positions): U.S. Forest Service (Forest Landscape Architect); EDSA (Land Planner); Design Workshop (Project Landscape Architect); State of Texas (Intergraph Computer Design); National Park Service (Field Landscape Architect); Araki Landscape Architects, Osaka, Japan (Landscape Architect)

NORWICH UNIVERSITY
Environmental Engineering Technology
Northfield, Vermont

Fast Facts About the Program
- **Established:** 1972
- **Enrollment:** 48
- **Faculty:** 4 (3 FT, 1 PT)
- **Student/Faculty Ratio:** 12:1
- **Degrees Conferred Since Inception:** 180
- **Degrees Conferred in 1991:** 11
- **Contact:** Gregory D. Wight, Department Chair, Environmental Engineering Technology Department, Norwich University, Northfield, VT 05663; phone 802-485-2256

Fast Facts About the School
- Independent comprehensive coed institution
- 1,125-acre campus in small-town setting
- **Enrollment:** 2,547
- **Faculty:** 207
- **Student/Faculty Ratio:** 14:1
- **Tuition and Fees:** $12,214
- **Room and Board:** $4776
- **Application Deadline:** Rolling
- **Entrance Difficulty Level:** Moderately difficult
- **Contact:** James M. Skinner, Director of Admissions, 802-485-2001

The Program
The program produces graduates who are trained to work with interdisciplinary environment evaluation teams of engineers, planners, chemists, and biologists. In the final 2 years, the emphasis is upon the applied aspects of environmental and industrial process measurement and evaluation through lectures, indoor laboratories, and in-the-field experience utilizing modern chemical, pollutant, and flow-rate monitoring equipment. Through structured laboratory experiments, students learn how to approach technological problems, apply measurement techniques, and interpret results. Graduate programs are available, and students may pursue a Master of Science degree in environmental engineering, health physics, and hazardous waste studies.

MAJOR/CONCENTRATIONS

Environmental Engineering Technology
Air Pollution Measurement
Hazardous Waste Disposal and
    Remediation
Noise Abatement
Radiation Monitoring/Protection
Solid-Waste Management
Water Pollution Control

Special Features
Students have access to modern laboratory equipment for air, water, noise, and radiation measurement. In their senior year, students are required to design and undertake a semester-long environmental measurement project. In the solid-waste area, a biweekly speaker series introduces students to current waste disposal issues. A weekly career seminar in the senior year helps students select a graduate school or pursue career opportunities.

The Result
Ninety-eight percent of graduates find employment in their field or enroll in graduate school within 6 months of graduation. They are working as air monitoring engineers, air pollution control engineers, health and safety engineers, environmental coordinators, chemists, air emission monitoring managers, asbestos removal coordinators, air consultants, wastewater division heads, water and sewerage superintendents, field chemists, hydrogeologists, air sampling project directors, technical sales representatives, water quality engineers, remediation engineering managers, environmental engineers, and chemical engineers.

PENNSYLVANIA STATE UNIVERSITY AT HARRISBURG–THE CAPITAL COLLEGE
Environmental Engineering Technology
Middletown, Pennsylvania

Fast Facts About the Program
- **Established:** 1967
- **Enrollment:** 72
- **Faculty:** 6 (3 FT, 3 PT)
- **Student/Faculty Ratio:** 12:1
- **Degrees Conferred Since Inception:** 350
- **Degrees Conferred in 1991:** 27
- **Contact:** Edwin Escalet, Director/Controller for Admissions, Admissions Building, Penn State Harrisburg, 777 W. Harrisburg Pike, Middletown, PA 17057; phone 717-948-6250

Fast Facts About the School
- State-related upper-level coed institution
- 218-acre campus in small-town setting
- **Enrollment:** 3,434
- **Faculty:** 178
- **Student/Faculty Ratio:** 14:1
- **Tuition:** State resident: $4332; nonresident: $9118
- **Fees:** $70
- **Room and Board:** $3670
- **Application Deadline:** Rolling
- **Entrance Difficulty Level:** Moderately difficult
- **Contact:** Edwin Escalet, Director/Controller for Admissions, 717-948-6250

The Program
The Environmental Engineering Technology Program at Penn State-Harrisburg provides a comprehensive education for students interested in pursuing a career in the environmental field. As one of 6 engineering technology programs offered

MAJOR

Environmental Engineering Technology

through the Division of Science, Engineering, and Technology, the program grants a Bachelor of Science degree in environmental engineering technology. ENV ET students take a broad range of courses that cover air, water, and solid- and hazardous-waste pollution; environmental chemistry; biology; management; and process design and operation.

Special Features
Penn State-Harrisburg is the only college in the state offering an accredited baccalaureate program in environmental engineering technology. The engineering technology division at Penn State-Harrisburg has been ranked among the largest of its kind in the country by the American Society for Engineering Education.

The Result
Penn State-Harrisburg ENV ET graduates have found positions in engineering consulting firms, industries, and public authorities. They function as designers, enforcement officials, reviewers, regulators, and site managers for water, wastewater, and solid- and hazardous-waste projects. ENV ET graduates are qualified to take the Engineering-In-Training (EIT) Examination.

Who's Recruiting Who on Campus
Employers: Pennsylvania Department of Environmental Resources, Gannett Fleming Engineers, CET Engineers, Buchart Horn, Envirep, U.S. Army Corps of Engineers, Roy F. Weston, Inc.

PURDUE UNIVERSITY
Environmental Engineering
West Lafayette, Indiana

Fast Facts About the Program	Fast Facts About the School
• **Established:** 1943 • **Enrollment:** 200 • **Faculty:** 6 (all FT) • **Student/Faculty Ratio:** 33:1 • **Degrees Conferred Since Inception:** 1,000 • **Degrees Conferred in 1991:** 45 • **Contact:** Ronald F. Wukasch, Professor, Civil Engineering, Purdue University, Lafayette, IN 47907; phone 317-494-2194	• State-supported coed university • 1,565-acre campus in suburban setting • **Enrollment:** 36,163 • **Faculty:** 2,208 • **Student/Faculty Ratio:** 18:1 • **Tuition:** State resident: $2324; nonresident: $7440 • **Room and Board:** $3010 • **Application Deadline:** Rolling • **Entrance Difficulty Level:** Moderately difficult • **Contact:** William J. Murray, Director of Admissions, 317-494-1776

The Program

The School of Civil Engineering has one of the pioneering environmental engineering programs in the world. This year, about one third of undergraduate students declaring an area of specialization in the School of Civil Engineering have selected environmental engineering. The graduate program, with more than 70 students, has also become the largest at the school.

> **MAJOR/CONCENTRATION**
>
> **Civil Engineering**
> Environmental Engineering

Special Features

Approximately 15,000 square feet of working space is available for research and instructional use. Specialized facilities for research include a pilot plant room; 8 constant-temperature rooms, including a walk-in freezer; a microbiology laboratory; and an air pollution laboratory. Students have the opportunity to attend and participate in the annual Purdue Industrial Waste Conference (PIWC), which has been sponsored by the school for more than 45 years. For 3 days in May, specialists from universities, consulting firms, industries, and regulatory agencies throughout the world gather at Purdue to attend and give nearly 100 technical papers.

The Result

Almost 100% of program graduates find jobs in their field or go on to advanced studies within 6 months of graduation. Environmental engineering alumni are leaders in industry, consulting companies, public and private utilities, and government agencies. Among alumni are heads of pollution control in companies such as Du Pont and Dow Corning. Many environmental service and consulting engineering firms and equipment manufacturing companies have been founded and nurtured into enterprises of national and international impact by former students.

Who's Recruiting Who on Campus

Most major U.S. corporations and agencies recruit at Purdue. In addition, a strong alumni-employer network provides upcoming graduates with job opportunities.

ROCHESTER INSTITUTE OF TECHNOLOGY
Civil Engineering Technology
Rochester, New York

Fast Facts About the Program
- **Established:** 1972
- **Enrollment:** 208
- **Faculty:** 7 (5 FT, 2 PT)
- **Student/Faculty Ratio:** 30:1
- **Degrees Conferred Since Inception:** 850
- **Degrees Conferred in 1991:** 52
- **Contact:** Robert H. Easton, Chairman, Civil Engineering Department, Rochester Institute of Technology, P.O. Box 9887, Rochester, NY 14623-9887; phone 716-475-2183

Fast Facts About the School
- Independent comprehensive coed institution
- 1,300-acre campus in suburban setting
- **Enrollment:** 13,018
- **Faculty:** 1,076
- **Student/Faculty Ratio:** 13:1
- **Tuition:** $12,525
- **Fees:** $195
- **Room and Board:** $5286
- **Application Deadline:** 7/1
- **Entrance Difficulty Level:** Moderately difficult
- **Contact:** Daniel Shelly, Director of Admissions, 716-475-6631

The Program
The program originated in 1972 as an upper-division program; in 1988, a lower-division component was added to accommodate entry at the freshman level. The objective of the program is to provide an academically demanding civil engineering technology education to students, while meeting the needs of industry with a group of applications-oriented graduates able to solve the challenging problems in today's society. The environmental component of the program includes instruction in waste management and water resources. A related course in land-use planning is offered. Students are required to accumulate 196 quarter hours of credit. This is accomplished in 12 academic quarters plus 5 quarters of cooperative education, spanning a total of 5 academic years.

MAJOR/CONCENTRATIONS
Civil Engineering Technology
Building and Heavy Construction
Construction Management
Environmental Controls
Structures
Water Resources

Special Features
The required cooperative education program starts during the spring quarter of the junior year. Students are required to work for wages in a field of endeavor related to academic areas of interest and personal preference. The Placement Office assists in securing job leads and interviews and conducts a series of training seminars to help students prepare for the job search process.

The Result
Graduates of the program are sought by a wide range of employers in a variety of positions spanning the civil engineering technology field. Job titles of recent graduates include field engineer, civil engineer, highway engineer, project engineer, staff engineer, assistant project manager, assistant superintendent, and junior engineer. Starting salaries in 1990 (the most recent data available) ranged from $17,000 to $41,000. More than 90% of graduates find employment in their field or enroll in graduate school within 6 months of graduation.

ROCHESTER INSTITUTE OF TECHNOLOGY
Packaging Science
Rochester, New York

Fast Facts About the Program
- **Established:** 1973
- **Enrollment:** 175
- **Faculty:** 7 (5 FT, 2 PT)
- **Student/Faculty Ratio:** 25:1
- **Degrees Conferred Since Inception:** 800
- **Degrees Conferred in 1991:** 60
- **Environmental Library Holdings:** 250 bound volumes; 6–10 periodical subscriptions; 30 records/tapes/CDs
- **Contact:** Dr. Daniel L. Goodwin, Chairman, Packaging Science Program, Rochester Institute of Technology, P.O. Box 9887, Rochester, NY 14623-9887; phone 716-475-2278

Fast Facts About the School
- Independent comprehensive coed institution
- 1,300-acre campus in suburban setting
- **Enrollment:** 13,018
- **Faculty:** 1,076
- **Student/Faculty Ratio:** 13:1
- **Tuition:** $12,525
- **Fees:** $195
- **Room and Board:** $5286
- **Application Deadline:** 7/1
- **Entrance Difficulty Level:** Moderately difficult
- **Contact:** Daniel Shelly, Director of Admissions, 716-475-6631

The Program
The mission of the program is to provide a comprehensive, broadly based, interdisciplinary undergraduate education that prepares students for entry-level professional employment in all facets of the packaging industry. The program is laboratory-based, utilizing state-of-the-art testing instruments. It is applications oriented, giving students hands-on experience. The study of packaging and container systems includes material selection, waste reduction, conservation, and recyclability. The goal of such study is to construct systems using minimal materials with maximal environmental protection.

MAJOR/CONCENTRATIONS

Packaging Science
Management Option
Printing Option
Technical Option

Special Features
The characteristics of the program include the following: it is career oriented, whereby graduates of the program are ready to enter directly into positions of responsibility; it is interdisciplinary, with the student becoming familiar with many facets of packaging through courses in several RIT colleges; it is flexible, as the program offers three options, management, technical, and printing, according to interest; it is representative of industry need, as content is developed with the assistance of the Rochester Area Packaging Association, consultants from the packaging industry, and educational specialists; and it is adaptable to a modified cooperative education plan used widely in other RIT programs. Two quarters of co-op work experience are required and can be scheduled at the student's convenience, following development of appropriate skills.

The Result
Typical jobs sought by graduates include work as packaging engineers, associate and junior packaging engineers, and sales engineers. Prospective employers come from the food, beverage, pharmaceutical, chemical, and many other industries. Opportunities for employment run the gamut and include jobs in design development, research, analysis, coordination, and service. Ninety percent of graduates find employment in their field or enroll in graduate school within 6 months of graduation.

TARLETON STATE UNIVERSITY
Hydrology and Water Resources
Stephenville, Texas

Fast Facts About the Program
- **Established:** 1983
- **Enrollment:** 48
- **Faculty:** 23 (22 FT, 1 PT)
- **Student/Faculty Ratio:** 2:1
- **Degrees Conferred Since Inception:** 35
- **Degrees Conferred in 1991:** 4
- **Contact:** Dr. Michael J. McLatchy, Director, Tarleton State University, Stephenville, TX 76402; phone, 817-968-9863

Fast Facts About the School
- State-supported comprehensive coed institution
- 120-acre campus in small-town setting
- **Enrollment:** 6,420
- **Faculty:** 309
- **Student/Faculty Ratio:** 22:1
- **Tuition:** State resident: $720; nonresident: $4860
- **Fees:** $700
- **Room and Board:** $2600
- **Application Deadline:** 8/15
- **Entrance Difficulty Level:** Moderately difficult
- **Contact:** Gail Mayfield, Director of Admissions, 817-968-9125

The Program
The Hydrology and Water Resources Program prepares the professionals are needed to solve the problems of transporting water in sufficient quantities and appropriate quality to where it is needed.

> **MAJOR**
> **Hydrology and Water Resources**

In 1991, the Texas Board of Registration for Professional Engineers accepted the Hydrology and Water Resources Program at Tarleton State University as the only non–ABET accredited program in the state that would qualify its graduates to take the first exam leading to eventual registration as professional engineers. Each year, the Phillip and Ruth Bratton Scholarship is awarded to a student majoring in the program. The recipient's award is $750 per semester. Students in the major must also complete a 9- to 13-week internship with a company or agency that has some experience in hydrology.

Special Features
There is an advisory council of water professionals that meets at least annually to review the Hydrology and Water Resurces Program. Their service is valuable in keeping the program current, and the acceptance of the program by the Board of Registration is but one example of the results of their efforts. Speakers from the Texas Water Conservation Association, the Brazos River Authority, the Texas Water Commission, the Texas Water Development Board, and the Edwards Underground District have visited the campus. The internship feature of the program puts students in direct contact with prospective employers.

The Result
Several graduates work for state or quasi-state agencies, including the Lower Colorado River Authority and the Texas Water Commission. Some have returned to Tarleton to work for the Texas Institute for Applied Enviromental Research. Some have pursued advanced degrees in environmental engineering. Ninety-five percent of graduates find employment or enroll in graduate school within 6 months of graduation.

UNIVERSITY OF CENTRAL FLORIDA
Environmental Engineering
Orlando, Florida

Fast Facts About the Program
- **Established:** 1967
- **Enrollment:** 172
- **Faculty:** 16 (all FT)
- **Student/Faculty Ratio:** 11:1
- **Degrees Conferred Since Inception:** 259
- **Degrees Conferred in 1991:** 15
- **Contact:** Dr. A. Essam Radwan, Chairperson, Civil and Environmental Engineering, ENG 307, University of Central Florida, Orlando, FL 32816; phone 407-823-2841

Fast Facts About the School
- State-supported coed university
- 1,227-acre campus
- **Enrollment:** 21,157
- **Faculty:** 1,143
- **Student/Faculty Ratio:** 17:1
- **Tuition:** State resident: $1442; nonresident: $5580
- **Fees:** $82
- **Room and Board:** $3909
- **Application Deadline:** 3/15
- **Entrance Difficulty Level:** Moderately difficult
- **Contact:** Jeanne Rutenkrocer, Interim Director of Admissions, 407-823-2511

The Program

The program began with the goal of educating students about the interaction of man and the environment. In the early years, students were educated in the planning, design, and control of systems for

MAJOR
Environmental Engineering

environmental quality management with an emphasis on the water environment. In recent years, all aspects of the environment have been incorporated. The program is accredited by the Accreditation Board for Engineering and Technology (ABET). Outstanding students are recruited by faculty members to assist in funded research projects.

Special Features

The program offers a number of lab courses, including those for studying wastewater microbiology, water chemistry, air pollution, hydrology, and hydraulics. Courses routinely require the use of personal computers, and computer facilities are readily available for student use. Several courses include field trips to local facilities, such as the Iron Bridge wastewater treatment plant, Orlando Utilities Commission coal-fired power plant, and Orange County Landfill.

The Result

About one third of the graduates take jobs with local, state, or federal government agencies. Almost half go to work for environmental engineering consulting firms. A few take jobs directly with industry, and some students go on to graduate school. Students have recently been hired by such companies as Radian Corp.; Camp Dresser & McKee; Professional Engineering Consultants; Grove Scientific; Engineering-Science; Howard, Needles, Tammen and Bergendorf; James Montgomery, Inc.; and CH2M Hill. Governmental agencies that have hired graduates in the last few years include the South Florida Water Management District, the Florida Highway Administration Bureau of the Environment, and Broward County Environmental Protection Department.

UNIVERSITY OF MASSACHUSETTS AT AMHERST
Environmental Design
Amherst, Massachusetts

Fast Facts About the Program	Fast Facts About the School
• **Established:** 1969 • **Enrollment:** 45 • **Faculty:** 9 (7 FT, 2 PT) • **Student/Faculty Ratio:** 5:1 • **Degrees Conferred Since Inception:** 1,200 • **Degrees Conferred in 1991:** 15 • **Contact:** Jack Ahern, Associate Professor, Program Director, 109 Hills North, University of Massachusetts at Amherst, Amherst, MA 01003; phone 413-545-6632	• State-supported coed university • 1,273-acre campus in small-town setting • **Enrollment:** 22,070 • **Faculty:** 1,223 • **Student/Faculty Ratio:** 18:1 • **Tuition:** State resident: $2052; nonresident: $7920 • **Fees:** $2811 • **Room and Board:** $3587 • **Application Deadline:** 2/15 • **Entrance Difficulty Level:** Moderately difficult • **Contact:** Timm R. Rinehart, Director, Undergraduate Admissions, 413-545-0222

The Program

To prepare students for the effective land-use decision-making process, the Environmental Design Program was started in 1969. The program offers students the opportunity to pursue a broad-based undergraduate education with an environmental focus. Its curriculum consists of 6 general education courses, a core of 7 environmental design courses, and an area of concentration comprising 8 courses. The University also offers a program in environmental sciences.

MAJOR/CONCENTRATIONS

Environmental Design
Architecture (nonprofessional)
Horticulture
Landscape Architecture (nonprofessional)
Landscape Planning
Student-Initiated Interdisciplinary Option
Urban and Regional Planning

Special Features

The Environmental Design program is supported by the following on-campus features: the University Computer Center, with geographic information systems (GIS) databases and statistical and graphics software capabilities; the University Research Forest; and the Five-College Consortium, which enables students to take courses and use libraries and other facilities at Amherst College, Smith College, Mt. Holyoke College, and Hampshire College. The University offers active study-abroad programs with the University of Scheffield in England and the Danish International Study Program in Copenhagen, Denmark.

The Result

Seventy percent of graduates find employment or enroll in graduate school within 6 months of graduation.

Who's Recruiting Who on Campus

Employers (Positions): Massachusetts Department of Environmental Management (State Forest Manager, Staff Planners); Massachusetts Geographic Information System (Foremen, Managers, Consultants); Peace Corps

---

UNIVERSITY OF MISSOURI–COLUMBIA
Civil Engineering
Columbia, Missouri

Fast Facts About the Program
- **Established:** 1849
- **Enrollment:** 165
- **Faculty:** 14 (all FT)
- **Student/Faculty Ratio:** 12:1
- **Degrees Conferred Since Inception:** 889
- **Degrees Conferred in 1991:** 47
- **Environmental Library Holdings:** 72,000 bound volumes; 600 periodical subscriptions
- **Contact:** Dr. Jay B. McGarraugh, Associate Chair, Undergraduate Programs, Engineering Complex, University of Missouri–Columbia, Columbia, MO 65211; phone 314-882-4688

Fast Facts About the School
- State-supported coed university
- 1,335-acre campus in small-town setting
- **Enrollment:** 24,660
- **Faculty:** 1,804
- **Tuition:** State resident: $2442 to $3282; nonresident: $7302 to $8142
- **Fees:** $370
- **Room and Board:** $3160
- **Application Deadline:** 5/15
- **Entrance Difficulty Level:** Moderately difficult
- **Contact:** Georgeanne Porter, Director, Undergraduate Admissions, 314-882-7786

The Program

Civil engineering was first taught at the University in 1849, giving it the distinction of being the first institution west of the Mississippi River to offer an engineering education. There are over 11 named scholarship sources available to civil engineering students. The program is accredited by ABET and course work consists of 126 hours. A minimum GPA of 2.0 is required overall, as it is for civil engineering courses.

MAJOR/CONCENTRATIONS
Construction Management and Planning
Hydraulic Engineering and Water Resources
Municipal and Public Works Engineering
Sanitary and Environmental Engineering
Structural Engineering
Transportation and Urban Systems Engineering

Special Features

The department is well equipped with advanced surveying equipment, and extensive laboratories are available for concrete and steel materials testing, soils testing, hydraulics and fluid mechanics, and chemical and microbiological analysis related to water supply and wastewater treatment. The program is highly laboratory oriented. Excellent shop facilities and technicians are available to fabricate and maintain the laboratory and research equipment.

The Result

Graduates work for consulting firms, contractors, and construction engineering and management companies in the private sector and for municipalities and state agencies. Some continue on at University of Missouri–Columbia or return later for master's and doctoral degrees in civil engineering.

Who's Recruiting Who on Campus

Employers: Missouri Highway and Transportation Department, B&V Waste Science and Technology, Illinois Department of Transportation, Black & Veatch, Burns and McDonnell, Missouri Department of Natural Resources, Federal Highway Administration, Bibb & Associates, U.S. Army Corps of Engineers, California Department of Transportation

WILKES UNIVERSITY
Environmental Engineering
Wilkes-Barre, Pennsylvania

Fast Facts About the Program	Fast Facts About the School
• **Established:** 1985 • **Enrollment:** 45 • **Faculty:** 8 (7 FT, 1 PT) • **Student/Faculty Ratio:** 6:1 • **Degrees Conferred Since Inception:** 25 • **Degrees Conferred in 1991:** 10 • **Contact:** Dale Bruns, Chair/Professor, Department of GeoEnvironmental Sciences and Engineering, Wilkes University, Wilkes-Barre, PA 18766; phone 717-831-4614	• Independent comprehensive coed institution • 25-acre campus in urban setting • **Enrollment:** 3,432 • **Faculty:** 219 • **Student/Faculty Ratio:** 13:1 • **Tuition:** $9500 • **Fees:** $368 • **Room and Board:** $4500 • **Application Deadline:** Rolling • **Entrance Difficulty Level:** Moderately difficult • **Contact:** Emory Guffrovich, Dean of Admissions, 717-831-4400

The Program

The Department of GeoEnvironmental Sciences and Engineering offers both 4- and 5-year degree programs in environmental engineering. The mission of these programs is to provide students with strong engineering and scientific experience using advanced techniques that have been heavily integrated into the curriculum. Students intending to major in these programs are encouraged to be well prepared in the sciences and mathematics.

MAJOR/CONCENTRATIONS

Environmental Engineering
Air and Water Quality Engineering
Hazardous-Waste Management
Hydrology
Others

Special Features

Special features include 2 water-quality laboratories with atomic absorption spectroscopy, UV-VIS spectroscopy, and portable field analysis instrumentation; an air quality laboratory with meteorological equipment and a Miran (IR) portable organic vapor analyzer; a gas chromatography/mass spectroscopy laboratory; a rock and mineral laboratory with mineral collection; CADD and CAE laboratories; a plant herbarium; insect/invertebrate collections; a 120-acre field research station with a solar-designed environmental home, lake, fields, stream, and forest habitats; an astronomy observatory; a natural floodplain forest on the Susquehanna River; and wetlands natural areas. Students are encouraged to participate in cooperative education or internships with agencies and industry. A senior research project is required on a relevant topic in environmental engineering design. Career advisement and Engineering-in-Training (EIT) test preparation are part of the required course work.

The Result

Currently, students are pursuing various graduate environmental engineering degree programs at institutions such as Clemson University and the Pennsylvania State University. Students also have been placed in industry and with consulting companies. Eighty to 90% of graduates find employment or enroll in graduate school within 6 months of graduation.

Environmental Health

A technical discipline within the overall field of allied health care, the environmental health profession seeks causes and solutions to threats to public health resulting from hazardous wastes, toxic chemicals, air and water pollution, and other environmental problems.

BOWLING GREEN STATE UNIVERSITY
Environmental Health
Bowling Green, Ohio

Fast Facts About the Program
- **Established:** 1973
- **Enrollment:** 60
- **Faculty:** 7 (3 FT, 4 PT)
- **Student/Faculty Ratio:** 9:1
- **Degrees Conferred Since Inception:** 200
- **Degrees Conferred in 1991:** 11
- **Contact:** Dr. Gary Silverman, Director, Environmental Health Department, Room 102 Health Center, Bowling Green State University, Bowling Green, OH 43403-0280; phone 419-372-7774

Fast Facts About the School
- State-supported coed university
- 1,176-acre campus in small-town setting
- **Enrollment:** 17,960
- **Faculty:** 913
- **Student/Faculty Ratio:** 20:1
- **Tuition:** State resident: $2506; nonresident: $6724
- **Fees:** $554
- **Room and Board:** $2686
- **Application Deadline:** Rolling
- **Entrance Difficulty Level:** Moderately difficult
- **Contact:** John W. Martin, Director of Admissions, 419-372-2086

The Program
Bowling Green State University provides students with both a liberal arts and a science-based technical education. The small size of its Environmental Health Program (limited to 60 majors) enhances the undergraduate experience and gives students the opportunity for substantial interaction with program faculty and hands-on experience.

MAJOR/CONCENTRATIONS
Environmental Health
Environmental Protection
Industrial Hygiene
Public Health

Special Features
BGSU's program is highly selective. It is one of only 22 programs accredited by the National Environmental Health Science and Protection Accreditation Council. The program has an active advisory council composed of representatives from government and industry. Students fulfill their internship requirement through diverse jobs across the country.

The Result
Eighty percent of graduates find employment in their field or enroll in graduate school within 6 months of graduation. Most enter the work force immediately. Many work as environmental protection specialists for public agencies in areas including air quality control, water quality control, hazardous-material management, site remediation, and sanitation. Others work for private industry as environmental managers, industrial hygienists, and consultants. Those students pursuing graduate degrees may enter traditional programs, or they may enter emerging programs in a field like hazardous-waste management. The curriculum is well suited to preparation for study in law and medicine.

Who's Recruiting Who on Campus
Employers (Positions): Ohio Environmental Protection Agency (Environmental Specialists); Hull and Associates Consulting Engineers (Environmental Consultants); U.S. Public Health Service (Public Health Sanitarians, Industrial Hygienists)

COLORADO STATE UNIVERSITY
Environmental Health
Fort Collins, Colorado

Fast Facts About the Program	Fast Facts About the School
• **Established:** 1969 • **Enrollment:** 130 • **Faculty:** 10 (all FT) • **Student/Faculty Ratio:** 13:1 • **Degrees Conferred Since Inception:** 375 • **Degrees Conferred in 1991:** 23 • **Contact:** Kenneth D. Blehm, Director of Curriculum, B120 Microbiology, Department of Environmental Health, Colorado State University, Fort Collins, CO 80523; phone 303-491-1406	• State-supported coed university • 833-acre campus in urban setting • **Enrollment:** 20,967 • **Faculty:** 1,019 • **Student/Faculty Ratio:** 20:1 • **Tuition:** State resident: $1855; nonresident: $6558 • **Fees:** $507 • **Room and Board:** $3624 • **Application Deadline:** 7/1 • **Entrance Difficulty Level:** Very difficult • **Contact:** Mary Ontiveros, Director of Admissions, 303-491-6909

The Program
The mission of this program is to produce competent, practicing field professionals in the areas of general environmental sanitation, industrial hygiene, epidemiology, toxicology, and waste management utilizing a combination of classroom and laboratory experiences and selected field projects as part of the mandated course work. The program draws on required internships with industry, government, and research institutions—coupled with many field practice opportunities—to produce students who can translate classroom knowledge into practical and effective solutions to environmental problems. Students involved in this program are supported by the Chirons Circle Scholarship Award to an outstanding candidate (renewable for each of 4 years of study), which is given by the Colorado Environmental Health Association Scholarship Award and by the Jim DeField Memorial Fellowship in industrial hygiene.

MAJOR/CONCENTRATIONS

Environmental Health
  Ecology
  Epidemiology
  Industrial Hygiene
  Toxicology
  Waste Management

Special Features
On-campus facilities include the Occupational Health and Safety Section laboratory and field investigation section where students gain valuable experience using state-of-the-art monitoring equipment and by accompanying health and safety professionals on consultation visits. The Center for Toxicology provides an excellent opportunity to become involved in pharmacologically based pharmacokinetics work, classical toxicology assessments, and similar activities. The department maintains the Advanced Systems Laboratory for Geographical Information Systems and over $750,000 in annually funded research. Finally, the department maintains an active summer employment and internship programming effort for students to work with business, industry, and government agencies.

Who's Recruiting Who on Campus
Employers: Los Alamos National Laboratories, INTEL Corporation, Tri-County District Health Department, Colorado Department of Health, Morrison-Knudsen, ENSR Environmental, Conoco, U.S. Corp of Engineers, ARCO Petroleum, Hewlett Packard. **Positions:** Sanitarian, Industrial Hygienist, Toxicologist, Epidemiologist.

EAST CAROLINA UNIVERSITY
Environmental Health
Greenville, North Carolina

Fast Facts About the Program
- **Established**: 1972
- **Enrollment**: 40
- **Faculty:** 6 (4 FT, 2 PT)
- **Student/Faculty Ratio:** 7:1
- **Degrees Conferred Since Inception:** 300
- **Degrees Conferred in 1991:** 15
- **Contact:** Dr. Y. J. Lao, Professor and Chairman, Department of Environmental Health, East Carolina University, Greenville, NC 27858; phone 919-757-4429

Fast Facts About the School
- State-supported coed university
- 460-acre campus in urban setting
- **Enrollment:** 16,690
- **Faculty:** 1,092
- **Tuition:** State resident: $676; nonresident: $5730
- **Fees:** $578
- **Room and Board:** $2710
- **Application Deadline:** 2/15
- **Entrance Difficulty Level:** Moderately difficult
- **Contact:** Dr. Thomas Powell Jr., Director of Admissions, 919-757-6640

The Program
The department offers Bachelor of Science and Master of Science degree programs. The programs prepare students to be highly competent registered and certified professionals. The curriculum consists of 2 phases: 2 years in General College and the junior and senior years, which make up the professional phase of the program. The minimum requirement for the Bachelor of Science degree is 126 semester hours of course work.

MAJOR/CONCENTRATIONS

Environmental Health
Industrial Hygiene
Public Health

Special Features
The Department of Environmental Health is situated in the School of Allied Health Sciences. The physical plant is located in a single building, where the common support services of AV equipment are available and a growing computer capability is offered. The department has 2 laboratories totaling 1,700 square feet. The department has more than $50,000 in major instruments, which include a gas chromatograph, an atomic absorption spectrophotometer, and a Miran IR gas analyzer. In addition, industrial hygiene instruments are used in the laboratory to train students. Environmental health majors are encouraged to take part in internships or become involved in the Cooperative Education Program.

The Result
The environmental health scientist works for the protection of air, food, and water and in industrial hygiene. Environmental surveillance and program administration are employed to ensure safe and sanitary conditions in public and private water supplies, food and drug processing concerns, food service establishments, recreational facilities, sewage disposal systems, and the workplace. Ninety-nine percent of graduates find employment in their field or enroll in graduate school within 6 months of graduation.

Who's Recruiting Who on Campus
Employers: State and county health departments and hospitals. **Positions:** Environmental Health Scientists and Specialists, Industry Hygienists.

FERRIS STATE UNIVERSITY
Industrial and Environmental Health Management
Big Rapids, Michigan

Fast Facts About the Program
- **Established:** 1964
- **Enrollment:** 155
- **Faculty:** 5 (3 FT, 2 PT)
- **Student/Faculty Ratio:** 31:1
- **Degrees Conferred Since Inception:** 750
- **Degrees Conferred in 1991:** 30
- **Contact:** Michael D. Ells, Associate Professor, Ferris State University, Big Rapids, MI 49307-2295; phone 616-592-2295

Fast Facts About the School
- State-supported comprehensive coed institution
- 650-acre campus in small-town setting
- **Enrollment:** 12,461
- **Faculty:** 709
- **Student/Faculty Ratio:** 17:1
- **Tuition:** State resident: $2565; nonresident: $5235
- **Fees:** $30
- **Room and Board:** $3318
- **Application Deadline:** Rolling
- **Entrance difficulty level:** Minimally difficult
- **Contact:** Dr. Duncan Sargent, Dean of Enrollment Services, 616-592-2100

The Program

The purpose of this curriculum is to train general environmental health, hazardous-waste management, industrial hygiene, and industrial safety professionals for local, state, and national governmental agencies and for industry. Freshmen are required to declare a major and begin their technical course work their first year.

MAJOR/CONCENTRATIONS
Industrialized Environmental Health Management
General Environmental Health
Hazardous-Waste Management
Industrial Hygiene
Industrial Safety

Special Features
The program has 2 specialty laboratories. A 10-week internship with a governmental agency or industry is mandatory. A required summer program, the Environmental Management Studies Block, is a 10-week capstone experience in which local communities request complete environmental and community assessments of their lake or river ecosystems. Students have organized the Ferris Industrial and Environmental Health Association (FIEHA), a chapter of the Student National Environmental Health Association, which has been awarded the outstanding Student Affiliate in the Nation award ten times in the past 17 years.

The Result
More than 95% of graduates find employment in local, state, and national health agencies and businesses within 6 months of graduation. FSU recommends that students begin graduate school only after completing 3 years of field experience.

Who's Recruiting Who on Campus
Employers (Positions): Ebasco Environmental Services (Environmental Specialist); Bechtel (Industrial Hygenist); Superior Environmental (Environmental Health and Safety Inspector); State of Montana (Sanitarian, Air Quality Specialist); Holland American Lines (Cruise Ship Sanitarian); Bremerton-Kitsap County Health Department (Sanitarian); Portage Co. (Sanitarian); Toledo City Health Department (Sanitarian)

OHIO UNIVERSITY
Environmental Health Science Program
Athens, Ohio

Fast Facts About the Program
- **Established:** 1975
- **Enrollment:** 61
- **Faculty:** 7 (4 FT, 3 PT)
- **Student/Faculty Ratio:** 9:1
- **Degrees Conferred Since Inception:** 125
- **Degrees Conferred in 1991:** 11
- **Contact:** Dr. Franklin B. Carver, Program Coordinator, 406W The Tower, Ohio University, Athens, OH 45701; phone 614-593-2134 or 4675

Fast Facts About the School
- State-supported coed university
- 700-acre campus in small-town setting
- **Enrollment:** 17,500
- **Faculty:** 940
- **Student/Faculty Ratio:** 21:1
- **Tuition:** State resident: $2967; nonresident: $6312
- **Room and Board:** $3633
- **Application Deadline:** 3/15
- **Entrance Difficulty Level:** Moderately difficult
- **Contact:** N. Kip Howard, Director of Admissions, 614-593-4100

The Program

The goal of the Environmental Health Science Program is to create environmental health science practitioners who can provide effective service to public health agencies, industries, and organiza-

MAJOR

Environmental Health Science

tions. Begun in 1975, the program was restructured and expanded from 1984 to 1990. Ohio University's program is now one of only 22 nationally accredited environmental health science programs. Many scholarships from several sources are available to undergraduates. Ohio University also offers a program in environmental geology.

Special Features

Learning resources are provided to students through the University library, including instructional media, equipment distribution, graphics and photographic services, and media production. A new instructional facility, the Tower, houses all health science faculty and many classrooms.

The Result

Graduates find employment with state and local health departments, federal and state agencies, private employers in quality control and regulation positions, the food and drug industry, the health-care industry, insurance companies and private consulting firms. Most students seek employment upon graduation in order to gain valuable work experience before pursuing a graduate degree; however, the program adequately prepares students to enter graduate and professional programs. About 90% of majors within this program find a job in their field or go on to pursue an advanced degree within 6 months of graduation.

Who's Recruiting Who on Campus

Employers: Ohio Environmental Protection Agency, Ohio Department of Health, U.S. Department of Agriculture, U.S. Department of the Navy, National Railroad Passenger Corp.–AMTRAK, Ford Motor Co., Westinghouse Electric Corp., Duke Power Co.

UNIVERSITY OF CALIFORNIA, DAVIS
Environmental Toxicology
Davis, California

Fast Facts About the Program
- **Established:** 1976
- **Enrollment:** 124
- **Faculty:** 8 (6 FT, 2 PT)
- **Student/Faculty Ratio:** 16:1
- **Degrees Conferred Since Inception:** 500
- **Degrees Conferred in 1991:** 41
- **Environmental Library Holdings:** 5,000 bound volumes; 100 periodical subscriptions
- **Contact:** Pam Fong, Advising Associate, Department of Environmental Toxicology, University of California, Davis, CA 95616; phone 916-752-1042

Fast Facts About the School
- State-supported coed university
- 6,010-acre campus in suburban setting
- **Enrollment:** 23,302
- **Faculty:** 1,626
- **Student/Faculty Ratio:** 19:1
- **Tuition:** State resident: $0; nonresident: $10,677
- **Fees:** $2979
- **Room and Board:** $5820
- **Application Deadline:** 11/30
- **Entrance Difficulty Level:** Very difficult
- **Contact:** Dr. Gary Tudor, Director of Admissions, 916-752-2971

The Program

The Environmental Toxicology (ETX) program at the University of California, Davis was the first of its kind in the country and abroad. Training at the undergraduate level consists of a major leading to a Bachelor of Science (B.S.) degree or a minor for students majoring in related fields. A curriculum consisting of 20 formal courses is offered. Man-made agents such as pesticides, industrial chemicals, food additives, and pollutants and naturally occurring toxic substances are covered. The scientific and legal bases for regulating toxic substances, public health, and environmental protection are also examined. Students can choose from specialty areas such as risk assessment, water quality, analysis, ecotoxicology, environmental chemistry, public/community health, and policy analysis.

MAJOR/CONCENTRATIONS

Environmental Toxicology
- Analysis
- Biochemical/Molecular Toxicology
- Ecotoxicology
- Environmental Chemistry
- Food Toxicology
- Policy Analysis
- Public/Community Health
- Risk Assessment
- Water Quality

Special Features

Program strengths are analytical and environmental chemistry, metabolism, biochemical mechanisms, and animal toxicology as applied to pesticides, industrial pollutants, mold toxins, and other natural and man-made poisons. Students have access to the Bodega Marine Lab. The Donald G. Crosby Summer Research Internship is a competitive 12-week program that provides a $3000 stipend and research experience.

The Result

Ninety-eight percent of graduates find employment or enroll in graduate school within 6 months of graduation. Jobs filled by graduates include: Chemical Control and Operations Manager in IBM's Research Division, Lab Research Technician at Cedars-Sinai Medical Center, assistant toxicologist/risk assessor for Emcon, and forensic investigator for the U.S. Department of Justice.

THE UNIVERSITY OF FINDLAY
Environmental and Hazardous Materials Management
Findlay, Ohio

Fast Facts About the Program
- **Established:** 1986
- **Enrollment:** 250
- **Faculty:** 12 (7 FT, 5 PT)
- **Student/Faculty Ratio:** 21:1
- **Degrees Conferred Since Inception:** 45
- **Degrees Conferred in 1991:** 20
- **Contact:** B. Michael Momany, Assistant to the Director, Environmental and Hazardous Materials Management, The University of Findlay, 1000 North Main Street, Findlay, OH 45840; phone 419-424-4502

Fast Facts About the School
- Independent comprehensive coed institution affiliated with Church of God
- 25-acre campus in small-town setting
- **Enrollment:** 2,896
- **Faculty:** 255
- **Student/Faculty Ratio:** 14:1
- **Tuition:** $8880
- **Fees:** $104
- **Room and Board:** $3930
- **Application Deadline:** Rolling
- **Entrance Difficulty Level:** Moderately difficult
- **Contact:** Mary Ellen Klein, Director of Admissions/Dean of Enrollment Management, 419-424-4540

The Program
The mission of the Environmental and Hazardous Materials Management Program is to foster education, training, and information transfer relevant to hazardous materials and general environmental concerns. The program offers A.A. and B.S. degrees, a certificate program in Environmental and Hazardous Materials Management, and a continuing education program in the Emergency Response Training Center facilities.

MAJOR/CONCENTRATIONS
Environmental and Hazardous Materials/Management
Biological Science
Environmental Health Physics
Environmental Management
General Science
Industrial Hygiene
Physical Sciences
Pre-Engineering

Special Features
Facilities include classrooms and laboratories with state-of-the-art instrumentation and a 5.5-acre training center with rail cars, tank trucks, line leak, drum leak, ditch/stream spill, and other scenarios. The summer job placement program has placed students with over 60 different companies.

The Result
Ninety-five to 100% of graduates find employment or enroll in graduate school within 6 months of graduation. Students have found jobs in project management, laboratory/compliance, health/safety/training, field services, and management/compliance. Six graduates of the program are in programs at Tufts University, Michigan State, and the University of Cincinnati.

Who's Recruiting Who on Campus
Employers: Westinghouse Environmental, Ohio EPA, Chem Waste Management, Marathon Oil Corp., OHM Corporation (Findlay), BASF Metcalf, and Eddy CBI

THE UNIVERSITY OF GEORGIA
Environmental Health Science
Athens, Georgia

Fast Facts About the Program
- **Established:** 1968
- **Enrollment:** 142
- **Faculty:** 4 (3 FT, 1 PT)
- **Student/Faculty Ratio:** 36:1
- **Degrees Conferred Since Inception:** 400
- **Degrees Conferred in 1991:** 18
- **Contact:** Dr. Harold Barnhart, Coordinator, Environmental Health Program, 206 Dairy Science Building, University of Georgia, Athens, GA 30602-2102; phone 706-542-2454

Fast Facts About the School
- State-supported coed university
- 1,601-acre campus in suburban setting
- **Enrollment:** 28,691
- **Faculty:** 1,982
- **Tuition:** State resident: $1722; nonresident: $5166
- **Fees:** $354
- **Room and Board:** $2988
- **Application Deadline:** 2/1
- **Entrance Difficulty Level:** Moderately difficult
- **Contact:** Dr. Claire Swann, Director of Admissions, 404-542-8776

The Program

The undergraduate program was initiated in 1968. The mission of the program is to give students a sound background in basic sciences and the fundamentals of environmental health. Through the

MAJOR
Environmental Health Science

appropriate selection of "special requirement" and elective courses, as well as the prudent use of free electives, students' special interests can be satisfied. A total of 192 quarter hours are required to complete the degree. Student financial aid is available through the university, and scholarships are available through the department, the college, and the University. Some scholarships are available through the national professional organization. Only departmental and professional organization scholarships are exclusively for environmental health students.

Special Features

Adjacent to the university campus is the Region 4 U.S. Environmental Protection Agency's Laboratory and the USDA Russell Research Center. Co-op and internship opportunities are developed with local, state, and federal agencies as well as industry. Students have contact with governmental agencies, business, and industry through seminars and speakers obtained for student organization activities.

The Result

An estimated 90% of graduates find employment or enroll in graduate school within 6 months of graduation. Graduates of the program have secured positions with local, state, and federal regulatory agencies, consulting firms, and private industry. Graduates go on to programs in toxicology, industrial hygiene, ecology, hazardous-waste management, and public health. They also enter professional programs such as medicine and veterinary medicine.

Who's Recruiting Who on Campus

Employers: Georgia Department of Natural Resources, Amoco Corp., Georgia Department of Human Resources, Lockheed Aeronautics, U.S. Environmental Protection Agency, ATSDR, Rollins Chempac Corp., Radian Corp. **Positions:** Environmental Specialist, Industrial Hygiene Specialist, Environmental Health Specialist.

WEST CHESTER UNIVERSITY
Environmental Health
West Chester, Pennsylvania

Fast Facts About the Program
- **Established:** 1978
- **Enrollment:** 40
- **Faculty:** 4 (all FT)
- **Student/Faculty Ratio:** 10:1
- **Degrees Conferred Since Inception:** 50
- **Degrees Conferred in 1991:** 10
- **Contact:** Betty Boyle, Chairperson, Department of Health, West Chester University, West Chester, PA 19383; phone 215-436-2931

Fast Facts About the School
- State-supported comprehensive coed institution
- 547-acre campus in small-town setting
- **Enrollment:** 11,959
- **Faculty:** 651
- **Student/Faculty Ratio:** 18:1
- **Tuition:** State resident: $2628; nonresident: $4892
- **Fees:** $310
- **Room and Board:** $3520
- **Application Deadline:** Rolling
- **Entrance Difficulty Level:** Moderately difficult
- **Contact:** Marsha Haug, Director of Admissions, 215-436-3411

The Program

The environmental health major is a comprehensive, applied science baccalaureate program. Students take 50 semester hours of science and math cognates and then 38 semester hours of applied science environmental course work. A senior internship is required.

MAJOR/CONCENTRATIONS

Environmental Health
Industrial Hygiene and Safety
Solid/Hazardous-Waste Management
Water Resources

Special Features

The program is supported by a state-of-the-art environmental analysis laboratory, equipped with a gas chromatograph, UV/VIS spectrophotometer, and a complete array of field monitoring and sampling equipment. The program also has a state-of-the-art Geographic Information System consisting of various programs and support hardware. A 100-acre natural area for field study is located on campus, and the program maintains affiliations with off-campus treatment facilities, industries, and field research stations.

The Result

Employers of graduates include environmental consulting firms, industry, federal and state regulatory agencies, and local nonprofit agencies. Field and laboratory technicians, pollution control compliance inspectors, industrial hygienists, Haz-Mat response team members, and lead/asbestos abatement specialists are some of the job titles held by graduates. Graduates have been accepted at Johns Hopkins University, University of Pittsburgh, Rutgers University, and University of Pennsylvania. All students find employment or enroll in graduate school within 6 months of graduation.

Who's Recruiting Who on Campus

Employers: Du Pont, Environmental Protection Agency, Pennsylvania Department of Environmental Resources, Environmental Resources Management

---

WESTERN CAROLINA UNIVERSITY
Environmental Health Science
Cullowhee, North Carolina

Fast Facts About the Program
- **Established:** 1981
- **Enrollment:** 91
- **Faculty:** 4 (2 FT, 2 PT)
- **Student/Faculty Ratio:** 23:1
- **Degrees Conferred Since Inception:** 121
- **Degrees Conferred in 1991:** 15
- **Contact:** Dr. Gary C. Smith, Director, Environmental Health Science Program, Western Carolina University, Cullowhee, NC 28723; phone 704-227-7113

Fast Facts About the School
- State-supported comprehensive coed institution
- 260-acre campus in rural setting
- **Enrollment:** 6,372
- **Faculty:** 443
- **Student/Faculty Ratio:** 16:1
- **Tuition:** State resident: $676; nonresident: $5730
- **Fees:** $653
- **Room and Board:** $2310
- **Application Deadline:** 8/1
- **Entrance Difficulty Level:** Moderately difficult
- **Contact:** Drumont Bowman, Director of Admissions, 704-227-7317

The Program
The Environmental Health Science Program focuses on the education of undergraduates in public health, occupational health, and environmental protection. Students are required to take courses in chemistry, biology, mathematics, and statistics. Major requirements include courses in air and water quality, epidemiology, solid- and hazardous-waste management, industrial hygiene, and sanitation. Western Carolina's program is one of 24 accredited by the Accrediting Council of Environmental Health Science and Protection. Laboratory and field experiences are available in water quality, air quality, and independent study of pollution.

MAJOR/CONCENTRATIONS
Environmental Health Science
Biology
Chemistry
Industrial Hygiene
Industrial Safety
Public Health

Special Features
Each student is required to complete at least 1 and usually 2 internships with industries, regulatory agencies, the U.S. Public Health Service, consulting firms, or local health departments. Internship opportunities are varied. For example, each year the U.S. Public Health Service employs several student COSTEPs in places like Alaska, Arizona, and Montana. The school's location in the Great Smoky Mountains provides students with opportunities to study diverse terrestrial and aquatic ecosystems.

Who's Recruiting Who on Campus
Employers (Positions): Royal Insurance Company (Loss Control Specialists); Agency for Toxic Substances and Disease Registry (Toxic-Substances Inventory Specialists); U.S. Public Health Service (Indian Health Service Sanitarians); North Carolina Department of Environment, Health and Natural Resources (Environmental Health Specialists); Burlington Industries (Industrial Hygienists); U.S. Army Corps of Engineers (Water Quality Specialists, Industrial Hygienists); N.E.O. Corp. (Air Monitoring Specialists)

WRIGHT STATE UNIVERSITY
Environmental Health Sciences
Dayton, Ohio

Fast Facts About the Program
- **Established:** 1975
- **Enrollment:** 95
- **Faculty:** 12 (5 FT, 7 PT)
- **Student/Faculty Ratio:** 8:1
- **Degrees Conferred Since Inception:** 250
- **Degrees Conferred in 1991:** 15
- **Contact:** Dr. G. A. Burton Jr., Director, Environmental Health Sciences Program, Biological Sciences Department, Wright State University, Dayton, OH 45435; phone 513-873-2655

Fast Facts About the School
- State-supported coed university
- 645-acre campus in suburban setting
- **Enrollment:** 17,761
- **Faculty:** 950
- **Student/Faculty Ratio:** 20:1
- **Tuition:** State resident: $2694; nonresident: $5388
- **Room and Board:** $3363
- **Application Deadline:** 9/1
- **Entrance Difficulty Level:** Noncompetitive
- **Contact:** Ken Davenport, Director of Undergraduate Admissions, 513-873-2211

The Program
The purpose of the program is to train environmental health sciences professionals who can translate environmental concern into effective action. The curriculum provides students with a sound academic background as well as specialized training and experience. During the senior year, students may select from a variety of science electives to personalize their program.

> **MAJOR**
> Environmental Health Sciences

Special Features
The field internship program is operated in cooperation with environmental health agencies and industries. This special aspect of the program gives students a better idea of career interests and options in addition to providing valuable job experience.

The Result
A number of career options are available to the college graduate with a major in environmental health. Graduates are employed by a number of federal and international agencies. Many state agencies and local government departments also hire graduates. Environmental specialists are engaged in administration, consulting and planning, teaching, research, and field practice. Participation in active research programs directed by the biological sciences faculty enables students to prepare for graduate work and provides practical training in current techniques for environmental research. All students in this program find a job in their field or continue their education at the graduate level within 6 months of graduation.

Who's Recruiting Who on Campus
Employers: Aqua Tech Environmental Consultants, Environmental Sciences and Engineering, Envirotech Operating Services, PEI Associates, Regional Air Pollution Control Agency, Sandusky County Department of Public Health, Ohio Environmental Protection Agency, U.S. Environmental Protection Agency

Environmental Science

Environmental science is a basic science program that focuses the general study of biology, chemistry, physics, geology, geography, and other science disciplines on environmental issues.

ALLEGHENY COLLEGE
Department of Environmental Science
Meadville, Pennsylvania

Fast Facts About the Program
- **Established:** 1982
- **Enrollment:** 76
- **Faculty:** 17 (all FT)
- **Student/Faculty Ratio:** 4:1
- **Degrees Conferred Since Inception:** 225
- **Degrees Conferred in 1991:** 19
- **Contact:** Ms. Gayle W. Pollock, Director of Admissions, Box 5, Allegheny College, Meadville, PA 16335; phone 814-332-4351

Fast Facts About the School
- Independent 4-year coed college, affiliated with United Methodist Church
- 254-acre campus in small-town setting
- **Enrollment:** 1,858
- **Faculty:** 198
- **Student/Faculty Ratio:** 11:1
- **Tuition:** $13,800
- **Fees:** $260
- **Room and Board:** $4210
- **Application Deadline:** 2/15
- **Entrance Difficulty Level:** Moderately difficult
- **Contact:** Ms. Gayle W. Pollock, Director of Admissions, 814-332-4351

The Program
The department offers 2 undergraduate majors. Although both programs are based on a strong natural science foundation, an environmental science major emphasizes the technical aspects of environmental science, whereas an environmental studies major explores concerns related to public policy, resource economics, and environmental writing. The program is noteworthy for a particularly strong groundwater component.

MAJORS/CONCENTRATIONS
Environmental Science
  Biology
  Chemistry
  Computer Science
  Geology
  Mathematics
Environmental Studies
  Economics
  English
  Political Science

Special Features
Many off-campus facilities and opportunitites are supported by the program. Among them are a semester-long Program in Sustainable Development in Costa Rica, in which students investigate the ecological, social, and political aspects of sustainable development. Joint-degree programs are also available in environmental management, forestry, and marine biology. Locally, students have access to many field study sites: Bousson Experimental Forest, Allegheny National Forest, Canadohta Lake, Geneva wetlands, Presque Isle State Park, and Erie National Wildlife Refuge.

The Result
More than 55% of graduates find employment in their field or go on to advanced study within 6 months of graduation. Environmental science majors are prepared for graduate programs and careers in aquatic ecology, ecotoxicology, forestry, industrial hygiene, water resources, environmental engineering, entomology, hydrogeology, and oceanography. Environmental studies majors are likely to pursue graduate programs and careers involving the public, such as business administration, coastal zone management, counseling and guidance, environmental law, forestry, journalism, and law.

ANDERSON UNIVERSITY
Biological Sciences/Environmental Studies
Anderson, Indiana

Fast Facts About the Program
- **Established:** 1970
- **Enrollment:** 25
- **Faculty:** 5 (all FT)
- **Student/Faculty Ratio:** 5:1
- **Degrees Conferred Since Inception:** 120
- **Degrees Conferred in 1991:** 6
- **Contact:** Dr. Susan P. Speece, Chair, Department of Biological Sciences, 1100 East 5th Street, Anderson University, Anderson, IN 46012; phone 317-641-4332

Fast Facts About the School
- Independent comprehensive coed institution, affiliated with Church of God
- 100-acre campus in suburban setting
- **Enrollment:** 2,162
- **Faculty:** 119
- **Student/Faculty Ratio:** 17:1
- **Tuition:** $8780
- **Room and Board:** $3120
- **Application Deadline:** 9/1
- **Entrance Difficulty Level:** Moderately difficult
- **Contact:** Phil Fair, Director of Admissions, 317-641-4082

The Program

The intent of this program is to prepare students to effectively address issues facing the environment. They are exposed to a broad liberal arts program as well as field studies and sociopolitical issues that surround the world environmental problems. Stu-

MAJOR/CONCENTRATION

Biology
Environmental Studies

dents major in biology with an emphasis in environmental studies. They have the opportunity to take regularly scheduled courses and to create independent study courses.

Special Features

The campus is an attractive habitat for studying human impacts. A nearby state park is also used for field studies. In addition, the University has become involved in the restoration of a wetland ecosystem that will be turned into an educational environmental site. Students have participated in internships with the state and national park systems. Students also have the opportunity to study at the Indiana Dunes National Lake Shore. Within a 20-mile radius of campus, students can study a solar aquatic sanitation system, a recycling system, and a water quality control research station. Anderson is associated with the Au Sable Institute, where students can spend part of a summer taking field courses. The institute offers courses and programs in field ecology, field biology, land resources, water resources, and environmental studies.

The Result

Most students go on to advanced programs in ecology, entomology, and environmental studies; however, those who elect to enter the work force directly have been employed by the Nature Conservancy, state and national parks, recycling corporations, and environmental assessing corporations. Ninety percent of students find a job in their field or go on to pursue an advanced degree within 6 months of graduation.

Who's Recruiting Who on Campus

Employers: Nature Conservancy of Missouri and Minnesota, various recycling corporations

BOWLING GREEN STATE UNIVERSITY
Environmental Science
Bowling Green, Ohio

Fast Facts About the Program
- **Established:** 1969
- **Enrollment:** 127
- **Faculty:** 35 (30 FT, 5 PT)
- **Student/Faculty Ratio:** 4:1
- **Degrees Conferred Since Inception:** 350
- **Degrees Conferred in 1991:** 31
- **Environmental Library Holdings:** 10,000 bound volumes; 86 periodical subscriptions; 65 records/tapes/CDs
- **Contact:** Dr. Thomas B. Cobb, Director, Center for Environmental Programs, 153 College Park Office Building, Bowling Green State University, Bowling Green, OH 43403; phone 419-372-8207

Fast Facts About the School
- State-supported coed university
- 1,176-acre campus in small-town setting
- **Enrollment:** 17,960
- **Faculty:** 913
- **Student/Faculty Ratio:** 20:1
- **Tuition:** State resident: $2506; nonresident: $6724
- **Fees:** $554
- **Room and Board:** $2686
- **Application Deadline:** Rolling
- **Entrance Difficulty Level:** Moderately difficult
- **Contact:** John W. Martin, Director of Admissions, 419-372-2086

The Program
The program seeks to provide students with an interdisciplinary science background. Laboratory methods, field experiences, computer techniques, and other skills necessary for the resolution of specific environmental problems are emphasized.

Special Features
Students are encouraged to take an internship. An example is an established position with the U.S. Fish and Wildlife Service for a biology aide to work on a research vessel on Lake Erie. A distinguished speaker series brings environmental specialists to campus; there is a special environmental film series as well. A program for employment referral is available.

MAJOR/CONCENTRATIONS
Environmental Science
Chemical Environmental Analysis
Ecology
Energy Resources
Hazardous Materials
Marine Systems
Natural Resources
Physical Environment (Aerial Photography, Geographic Information Systems, Geomorphology, Hydrology)
Water Quality

The Result
Eighty-five percent of graduates find employment in their field or enroll in graduate school within 6 months of graduation. Recent placements have included positions in water quality management and analysis, site remediation and environmental analysis, regional health departments, corporate health and safety offices, hazard communications, regulatory affairs, and environmental consulting. About 20% of majors continue on to graduate school to pursue further study in hazardous materials management, environmental chemistry, solar energy, natural resource management, or ecology.

Who's Recruiting Who on Campus:
Employers: Ferro Corp., Bechtel Environmental, U.S. Department of Defense, North Regional Waste Water Treatment, City of Dayton, NASA Plum Brook Station, Ohio EPA, Standard & Poor's, Peace Corps, Glidden Co., Libbey-Owens-Ford Corp., H. S. Westover

BOWLING GREEN STATE UNIVERSITY
Environmental Science Education
Bowling Green, Ohio

Fast Facts About the Program
- **Established:** 1969
- **Enrollment:** 12
- **Faculty:** 35 (30 FT, 5 PT)
- **Degrees Conferred Since Inception:** 45
- **Degrees Conferred in 1991:** 4
- **Environmental Library Holdings:** 10,000 bound volumes; 86 periodical subscriptions; 65 records/tapes/CDs
- **Contact:** Dr. Adelia M. Peters, Advisor, Education Building, Bowling Green State University, Bowling Green, OH 43403

Fast Facts About the School
- State-supported coed university
- 1,176-acre campus in small-town setting
- **Enrollment:** 17,960
- **Faculty:** 913
- **Student/Faculty Ratio:** 20:1
- **Tuition:** State resident: $2506; nonresident: $6724
- **Fees:** $554
- **Room and Board:** $2686
- **Application Deadline:** Rolling
- **Entrance Difficulty Level:** Moderately difficult
- **Contact:** John W. Martin, Director of Admissions, 419-372-2086

The Program
The Environmental Science Education Program seeks to prepare students for teaching environmental/ecology courses in Ohio public and private secondary schools. The program provides students with the skills to teach others to understand the natural environment and to act in environmentally sound ways. Majors take advanced science courses in biology and professional courses in teaching skills. They are required to become proficient in mathematics, life sciences, and chemistry with an emphasis on laboratory procedures. All pursue course work leading to certification in biology and general science and must also select another science area for certification from earth science, chemistry, or physics.

MAJOR/CONCENTRATIONS
Environmental Science Education
Chemistry
Earth Science
Physics

Special Features
All students in this major serve a term of practice teaching under the guidance of an experienced teacher in the environmental studies/ecology or biology areas. A Distinguished Speakers Series brings well-known teachers to the BGSU campus to analyze environmental issues from a teacher's perspective.

The Result
Most graduates of this program are employed as teachers in middle, junior high, and senior high schools. Some work in nature centers, for alternative education programs like Outward Bound, in mentoring programs, in camps, and for the Peace Corps. The program places 85% of its graduates in a job related to their field or in advanced degree programs.

Who's Recruiting Who on Campus
The BGSU College of Education receives information about positions from school districts around the state as well as about positions in other states. School districts that need teachers in the sciences send recruiters to Bowling Green State.

CLARK UNIVERSITY
Environment, Technology, and Society
Worcester, Massachusetts

Fast Facts About the Program
- **Established:** 1984
- **Enrollment:** 25
- **Faculty:** 13 (12 FT, 1 PT)
- **Student/Faculty Ratio:** 2:1
- **Degrees Conferred Since Inception:** 200
- **Degrees Conferred in 1991:** 10
- **Environmental Library Holdings:** 8,000 bound volumes; 500 periodical subscriptions
- **Contact:** Richard W. Pierson, Dean of Admissions, Admissions House, Clark University, Worcester, MA 01610; phone 508-793-4333

Fast Facts About the School
- Independent coed university
- 50-acre campus in urban setting
- **Enrollment:** 2,885
- **Faculty:** 172
- **Student/Faculty Ratio:** 12:1
- **Tuition:** $15,800
- **Fees:** $380
- **Room and Board:** $4500
- **Application Deadline:** 2/15
- **Contact:** Richard W. Pierson, Dean of Admissions, 508-793-7431

The Program

The Environment, Technology, and Society (ETS) Program challenges students to limit the misuse and social costs of technology while preserving its benefits. The program is interdisciplinary and emphasizes policy questions involving the environ-

> **MAJOR**
>
> Environment, Technology, and Society

ment. The goal of the program is to enable students to deal with technical issues in a social and political context and to do so with an acute awareness of the short- and long-range limitations of the natural environment in its response to human intervention. The ETS Program offers an undergraduate major, Master of Arts degrees in environmental affairs and in technology assessment and risk analysis, and an individually designed Doctor of Philosophy degree.

Special Features

Students have use of the 8 college libraries in the Worcester Consortium and, through an on-line catalog, have access to the collections of 43 local libraries. CD-ROM databases are available in Goddard Library for researching citations to periodicals and journals. The Guy Burnham Map and Aerial Photography Library has a total of 181,000 maps and 7,300 aerial photographs, plus atlases, journals, globes, and map reference materials. Computer facilities include a cluster of DEC VAX computers, including a VAX 6310, a VAX 8530, and 2 VAX 11/750s. The Computer Mapping Laboratory has 10 Intel 80386–based computers with color monitors, 5 digitizing tables, and 5 laser-quality printers. The George Perkins Marsh Institute includes the Center for Technology, Environment, and Development (CENTED), which focuses on environmental hazards and risks as well as global change in 9 critical zones where environmental degradation threatens human well-being. The George Perkins Marsh Institute Library is one of North America's most extensive research collections on environmental change. The Arthur M. Sackler Sciences Center houses laboratories and state-of-the-art scientific equipment, such as an electron microscope and high-field NMR spectrometers. The Hadwen Arboretum, a 27-acre natural woodlot about 1 mile from campus, contains exotic trees and shrubs as well as native species.

COLLEGE OF THE ATLANTIC
Human Ecology
Bar Harbor, Maine

Fast Facts About the Program
- **Established:** 1969
- **Enrollment:** 230
- **Faculty:** 21 (15 FT, 6 PT)
- **Student/Faculty Ratio:** 11:1
- **Degrees Conferred Since Inception:** 500
- **Degrees Conferred in 1991:** 60
- **Contact:** Rich Borden, Academic Dean, College of the Atlantic, 105 Eden Street, Bar Harbor, ME 04609; phone 207-288-5015

Fast Facts About the School
- Independent comprehensive specialized coed institution
- 25-acre campus in small-town setting
- **Enrollment:** 253
- **Faculty:** 32
- **Student/Faculty Ratio:** 10:1
- **Tuition:** $12,300
- **Fees:** $145
- **Room and Board:** $3385
- **Application Deadline:** 3/1
- **Entrance Difficulty Level:** Moderately difficult
- **Contact:** Steve Thomas, Director of Admission and Financial Aid, 207-288-5015 Ext. 233

The Program
College of the Atlantic was founded in 1969 to provide an ecological problem-solving approach to education that combines academic rigor in the arts and sciences with practical application. The College's small size allows students to work closely with faculty to design an individualized program suited to their own particular interests.

Special Features
The College's library has 27,000 volumes and subscribes to 38 periodicals. Through the OCLC computer system for interlibrary loans, students have access to libraries throughout the United States, Great Britain, and Canada. COA has biology, chemistry, and saltwater labs; a chemical equipment room; design and ceramics studios; a solar-heated greenhouse; a student computer lab; and boats that are used for marine-related courses. Additionally, the oceanfront location of the campus allows students to take advantage of the abundant natural resources offered by the Atlantic Ocean and nearby Acadia National Park.

The Result
The career paths of COA graduates are remarkably varied. Approximately 45% of COA graduates go on to earn advanced degrees in the environmental sciences, public policy, architecture, health, law, education, psychological counseling, and religion. Others work as journalists, teachers, naturalists, conservationists, farmers, carpenters, planners, and administrators. A significant number of graduates start new businesses.

MAJOR/CONCENTRATIONS

Human Ecology
- Botany
- Ecology and Evolution
- Environmental Journalism
- Environmental Studies
- Fine Arts
- Humanities
- Landscape Design
- Marine Biology
- Museum Preparation
- Public Planning and Policy
- Teacher Education

CONCORDIA LUTHERAN COLLEGE
Environmental Science
Austin, Texas

Fast Facts About the Program
- **Established:** 1986
- **Enrollment:** 31
- **Faculty:** 5 (4 FT, 1 PT)
- **Student/Faculty Ratio:** 6:1
- **Degrees Conferred Since Inception:** 21
- **Degrees Conferred in 1991:** 5
- **Contact:** Dr. Laurence Meissner, Environmental Science Program Director, Concordia Lutheran College, 3400 North Highway 35, Austin, TX 78705; phone 512-452-7661

Fast Facts About the School
- Independent 4-year coed college, affiliated with Lutheran Church-Missouri Synod
- 20-acre campus in metropolitan setting
- **Enrollment:** 688
- **Faculty:** 65
- **Student/Faculty Ratio:** 16:1
- **Tuition:** $6000
- **Fees:** $240
- **Room and Board:** $3200
- **Application Deadline:** 8/15
- **Entrance Difficulty Level:** Minimally difficult
- **Contact:** Kurt M. Senske, Registrar-Admissions Officer, 512-452-7661 Ext. 145

The Program

Through cross-disciplinary course requirements and a special emphasis on problem solving and off-campus study, the school's goal is to instill in students a broad-based knowledge of the environment,

> **MAJOR**
> **Environmental Science**

positive attitudes toward conservation, and laboratory and field skills that prepare them for work in the environmental field or for graduate school.

Special Features

Ideally located in the ecological crossroad of Central Texas, Concordia has easy access to pine forests to the east, grasslands to the north, the desert to the west, and the neotropical valley and Gulf of Mexico to the South. Austin, the state's capitol, is an environmentally progressive city where students have interned in federal agencies such as the Army National Guard and the National Wildflower Research Center; state agencies such as the Water Commission and the Parks and Wildlife Department; city departments such as planning and environmental health; and private environmental consulting and monitoring corporations. Out-of-state sites frequently studied are the neotropical rain forests, the coral reefs of the Caribbean region, and the desert southwest areas of New Mexico, Arizona, and California.

The Result

Fifteen recent graduates are pursuing master's degrees in biology, geography, and urban and regional planning. Another is working as a Water Quality Specialist III with the Texas Water Commission in Beaumont. Seven are working for environmental consulting firms in Austin and Dallas doing environmental monitoring and Phase I environmental site assessment work. Ninety percent of graduates find employment or enroll in graduate school within 6 months of graduation.

🌲

DELAWARE VALLEY COLLEGE
Soils and Environmental Science
Doylestown, Pennsylvania

Fast Facts About the Program
- **Established:** 1988
- **Enrollment:** 72
- **Faculty:** 12 (6 FT, 6 PT)
- **Student/Faculty Ratio:** 6:1
- **Degrees Conferred Since Inception:** 14
- **Degrees Conferred in 1991:** 7
- **Contact:** Fred T. Wolford, Chairman, Department of Agronomy and Environmental Science, Delaware Valley College, 700 East Butler Avenue, Doylestown, PA 18901-2697; phone 215-345-1500 Ext. 2260

Fast Facts About the School
- Independent 4-year coed college
- 600-acre campus in surburban setting
- **Enrollment:** 1,204
- **Faculty:** 90
- **Student/Faculty Ratio:** 14:1
- **Tuition:** $9651
- **Fees:** $475
- **Room and Board:** $3900
- **Application Deadline:** Rolling
- **Entrance Difficulty Level:** Moderately difficult
- **Contact:** Stephen W. Zenko, Director of Admissions, 215-345-1500 Ext. 2211

The Program
Students receive a broad, comprehensive background in the environmental science field augmented by the selection of a track of professional courses leading to the degree. Program flexibility allows students to specialize in a particular field of interest while achieving their highest potential in preparation for graduate study. The curriculum includes a required off-campus employment program. There are an increasing number of scholarships and internships available for students in the major.

MAJOR/CONCENTRATIONS
Soils and Environmental Science
Ecology
Hydrology/Hydrogeology
Plant /Crop Science
Soil Science

Special Features
Adjacent to the main campus, there are over 500 acres of open land that include croplands, forests, wetlands, lakes and streams, and a wide variety of plant and animal life. These outdoor "laboratory" areas are used for instruction and research. Research projects are conducted in cooperation with major ag-chemical companies, the Bucks County Conservation District, the USDA, and others. Course work is supplemented by a 24-week off-campus employment program that provides each student with on-the-job experience. In addition, special projects and a senior research program are available for credit.

The Result
Virtually all graduates find employment in their field or pursue graduate work within 6 months of graduation. Examples of positions held by these majors include conservationists, soil scientists, ecologists, environmental scientists, land-use specialists, teachers and professors, and hazardous-waste managers.

Who's Recruiting Who on Campus
Employers (Positions): U.S. Department of Agriculture Soil Conservation Service (Soil Conservationist, Plant Protection, Quarantine Officer, Soil Scientist, Wildlife Biologist); Land-Tech Remedial Company (Environmental Technician); Enviro-Gro Technologies (Plant Production Specialist)

EAST CENTRAL UNIVERSITY
Environmental Science
Ada, Oklahoma

Fast Facts About the Program
- **Established:** 1970
- **Enrollment:** 85
- **Faculty:** 3 (all FT)
- **Student/Faculty Ratio:** 28:1
- **Degrees Conferred Since Inception:** 245
- **Degrees Conferred in 1991:** 14
- **Contact:** Dr. M. L. Rowe, Department Chair, Environmental Science, East Central University, Box N-4, Ada, OK 74820; phone 405-332-8000

Fast Facts About the School
- State-supported comprehensive coed institution
- 140-acre campus in small-town setting
- **Enrollment:** 4,388
- **Faculty:** 200
- **Student/Faculty Ratio:** 23:1
- **Tuition:** State resident: $1350; nonresident: $3480
- **Fees:** $150
- **Room and Board:** $1988
- **Application Deadline:** 8/19
- **Entrance Difficulty Level:** Moderately difficult
- **Contact:** Pamla Armstrong, Registrar, 405-332-8000 Ext. 234

The Program

East Central University offers a B.S. degree in environmental science. The program was established to educate undergraduates for entry-level positions with state and federal environmental agencies. The curriculum was later changed to provide the knowledge and skills required for environmental management positions. The University requires the completion of a minimum of 124 credit hours, including at least 50 credit hours in the Department of Environmental Science. Of those 50 hours, 42 must be regular didactic and laboratory courses. An 8-hour internship is required.

MAJOR/CONCENTRATIONS

Environmental Science
Environmental Health
Environmental Management
Industrial Hygiene
Water and Wastewater Technology

Special Features

The Department of Environmental Science is located in the Physical and Environmental Science Building. The University campus is close to the Robert S. Kerr Environmental Research Laboratory, which is an EPA facility and one of many internship sites available to undergraduates; several undergraduates work there as part-time employees.

The Result

Most graduates accept entry-level positions with state and federal agencies and private industry. The job titles most often used in these positions include sanitarian, environmental health specialist, environmental specialist, industrial hygienist, and environmental manager. Ninety percent of graduates find employment in their field or enroll in graduate school within 6 months of graduation.

Who's Recruiting Who on Campus

Employers (Positions): Indian Health Service (Sanitarians); Oklahoma State Department of Health (Environmental Health Specialists); Oklahoma State Department of Labor (Industrial Hygienists); Environmental Protection Agency (Environmental Specialists); Tulsa City-County Health Department (Environmental Health Specialists)

EASTERN CONNECTICUT STATE UNIVERSITY
Environmental Earth Science
Willimantic, Connecticut

Fast Facts About the Program
- **Established:** 1972
- **Enrollment:** 100
- **Faculty:** 10 (5 FT, 5 PT)
- **Student/Faculty Ratio:** 10:1
- **Degrees Conferred Since Inception:** 500
- **Degrees Conferred in 1991:** 20
- **Contact:** Dr. Henry I. Snider, Chair, Environmental Earth Science Department, Eastern Connecticut State University, 83 Windham Street, Willimantic, CT 06226; phone 203-456-5202

Fast Facts About the School
- State-supported comprehensive coed institution
- 100-acre campus in small-town setting
- **Enrollment:** 4,328
- **Faculty:** 195
- **Student/Faculty Ratio:** 19:1
- **Tuition:** State resident: $1518; nonresident: $4916; nonresident eligible for New England Regional Student Program: $2278
- **Fees:** $1170 for state residents and nonresidents eligible for New England Regional Student Program; $1958 for other nonresidents
- **Room and Board:** $3748
- **Application Deadline:** 5/1
- **Entrance Difficulty Level:** Moderately difficult
- **Contact:** Dr. Arthur C. Forst Jr., Director of Admissions and Enrollment Planning, 203-456-5286

The Program
The major offers a strong foundation in geology. The student takes a sequence of requisite earth science courses. Students then choose from 3 concentrations. Students interested in elementary or secondary school teaching can select the earth science concentration. Those who wish to emphasize environmental aspects with an interdisciplinary approach select the environmental concentration. Others who wish to focus on the geologic aspects select the geologic concentration. For all concentrations, additional study in earth science, biology, chemistry, computer science, mathematics, and physics is recommended.

MAJOR/CONCENTRATIONS
Environmental Earth Science
Earth Science
Environment
Geology

Special Features
Internships and independent study opportunities are available for advanced students. Cooperative Education (Co-op) is an optional work-study program in which students may complete one or more periods of cooperative employment experiences.

The Result
Past graduates have gone on to M.S. and Ph.D. programs in geology, natural resource management, and environmental health. Career opportunities include positions with the Connecticut Department of Environmental Protection and the U.S. Geologic Survey Water Resources Branch and in independent environmental and engineering consulting firms as entry-level environmental specialists (earth science).

EASTERN ILLINOIS UNIVERSITY
Environmental Biology
Charleston, Illinois

Fast Facts About the Program
- **Established:** 1972
- **Enrollment:** 160
- **Faculty:** 27 (25 FT, 2 PT)
- **Student/Faculty Ratio:** 6:1
- **Degrees Conferred Since Inception:** 600
- **Degrees Conferred in 1991:** 45
- **Contact:** Dr. Kipp C. Kruse, Professor and Chair, Environmental Biology Program, Eastern Illinois University, Charleston, IL 61920; phone 217-581-3363

Fast Facts About the School
- State-supported comprehensive coed institution
- 325-acre campus in small-town setting
- **Enrollment:** 10,450
- **Faculty:** 643
- **Student/Faculty Ratio:** 17:1
- **Tuition:** State resident: $1656 to $1680; nonresident: $4968 to $5040
- **Fees:** $676
- **Room and Board:** $2694
- **Application Deadline:** Rolling
- **Entrance Difficulty Level:** Moderately difficult
- **Contact:** Mr. Dale W. Wolf, Director, Admissions, 217-581-2223

The Program

The Environmental Biology Program uses an interdisciplinary approach in the field of biology with an emphasis on ecologically oriented training. As a result, students are given a solid and diverse background for working in most environmental positions. Besides extensive course work in botany, zoology, and environmental biology, students take courses in chemistry, economics, and geology to develop a broad background in most areas related to environmental science. All students enroll in an internship (generally in their senior year) that provides on-the-job training in some environmental capacity.

MAJOR/CONCENTRATIONS

Environmental Biology
Aquatic Biology
Fisheries Biology
Terrestrial Ecology

Special Features

Excellent facilities on campus and at nearby sites are available for study. Currently, Eastern Illinois owns 4 high-quality natural areas that are used for class field trips and research. As a result of the campus location at the edge of the terminal moraine of the last glacial period, the program also has access to 3 major naturally occurring divisions. In this area, a high diversity of habitats and organisms are found.

The Result

Graduates from the Environmental Biology Program at Eastern Illinois can be found from coast to coast working for private corporations and municipal, state, and federal conservation and environmental monitoring agencies. Examples of places of employment for alumni include state departments of transportation, state departments of conservation, state and federal environmental protection agencies, state water surveys, the U.S. Fish and Wildlife Service, the U.S. Forest Service, and the U.S. Army Corps of Engineers. Approximately 20% to 30% of alumni continue their education to receive graduate degrees. Between 80% and 90% of graduates find employment in their field or enroll in graduate school within 6 months of graduation.

FERRUM COLLEGE
Environmental Science
Ferrum, Virginia

Fast Facts About the Program
- **Established:** 1941
- **Enrollment:** 87
- **Faculty:** 19 (13 FT, 6 PT)
- **Student/Faculty Ratio:** 5:1
- **Degrees Conferred Since Inception:** 250
- **Degrees Conferred in 1991:** 25
- **Contact:** Dr. Joseph D. Stogner, Coordinator/Director of Environmental Sciences, Ferrum College, Ferrum, VA 24088; phone 703-365-4369

Fast Facts About the School
- Independent Methodist 4-year coed college
- 880-acre campus in rural setting
- **Enrollment:** 1,211
- **Faculty:** 98
- **Student/Faculty Ratio:** 15:1
- **Tuition:** $8120
- **Room and Board:** $3730
- **Application Deadline:** Rolling
- **Entrance Difficulty Level:** Moderately difficult
- **Contact:** Robert H. Bailey, Director of Admissions, 703-365-4290

The Program

The program was developed to provide environmentally trained graduates with broad technical and academic backgrounds. Successful graduates must complete a minimum of 127 semester hours in a curriculum that requires a minimum of 3 semesters of chemistry, 1 semester of statistics, an appropriate level of math, and a minimum 400-hour internship.

MAJOR/CONCENTRATIONS

Environmental Science
Engineering Design and Pollution Control
Forestry
Game and Wildlife Management
Occupational Safety and Health

Special Features

In aquatic classes, students use a 17-foot Boston Whaler research vessel equipped for limnological study. Also available are numerous natural habitats and settings unique to the College's location in southwest Virginia's Blue Ridge Mountains. A lake, 2 ponds, and acres of varied woodlands offer a wide range of field opportunities, as do 2 large reservoirs–25,000-acre Smith Mountain Lake and 2,200-acre Philpott Lake–located within a 20-minute drive of campus.

The Result

Approximately 25 to 30% of graduates enter graduate programs in ecology and/or engineering. All graduates find employment or enroll in graduate school within 6 months of graduation.

Who's Recruiting Who on Campus

Employers: Environmental Protection Agency, Department of the Interior, Army Corps of Engineers, Goode Environmental Services, Environmental Technologies, Earth Reach Environmental Consultants, the Research Triangle Institute

---

IDAHO STATE UNIVERSITY
B.S. in Ecology
Pocatello, Idaho

Fast Facts About the Program
- **Established:** 1985
- **Enrollment:** 145
- **Faculty:** 12 (all FT)
- **Student/Faculty Ratio:** 12:1
- **Degrees Conferred Since Inception:** 150
- **Degrees Conferred in 1991:** 37
- **Contact:** Dr. Rod R. Seeley, Chair, Department of Biological Sciences, Box 8007, Idaho State University, Pocatello, ID 83209; phone 208-236-3765

Fast Facts About the School
- State-supported coed university
- 274-acre campus in small-town setting
- **Enrollment:** 11,000
- **Faculty:** 464
- **Student/Faculty Ratio:** 16:1
- **Tuition:** State resident: $1230; nonresident: $3350
- **Room and Board:** $2600
- **Application Deadline:** 8/15
- **Entrance Difficulty Level:** Minimally difficult
- **Contact:** Ms. Jodi Anderson, Associate Director, Enrollment Planning and Academic Services, 208-236-3277

The Program
The undergraduate ecology major is designed to help students develop an understanding of ecological principles and emphasizes the collection and analysis of field data.

> **MAJOR**
> Ecology

Special Features
The program has active research sites at the Idaho National Engineering Laboratory (INEL), including studies on vegetation, insects, birds, small mammals, jackrabbits, coyotes, and pronghorn; Harriman State Park, which is located in a collapsed volcanic cone and focuses on trout fishery and the unique trumpeter swan population; O'Neal Ecological Reserve, which consists of about 200 acres of sagebrush-grassland, lava outcroppings, and riparian habitat; and Yellowstone and Grand Teton national parks, the Frank Church Wilderness Area, and Craters of the Moon National Monument. Other resources available to undergraduates include the Center for Ecological Research and Education (CERE), which supports collaborative research on a riparian ecosystem in Yellowstone; the Idaho Museum of Natural History, located on the ISU campus, which houses the Davis Herbarium, a vertebrate and insect collection, and one of the largest collections of fossils in the country; and the Malheur Consortium, a group of 22 colleges and universities that support the Malheur Field Station (MFS), which is located on the Malheur National Wildlife Refuge, a diverse setting of extensive marshlands, desert basins of alkali playas, uplands of desert scrub steppe, volcanic and glacial land forms, and fault block mountains.

The Results
Examples of positions held by ISU Ecology graduates include: Fisheries Project Leader for the Shoshone Bannock Tribes, Plant Ecologists for the Idaho Power Co., Hydrological Permit Specialist for the U.S. Fish and Wildlife Service, Fish Biologist for the Washington Water Power Co., and Ecologist for the Idaho National Engineering Laboratory.

INDIANA STATE UNIVERSITY
Environmental Geography and Environmental Geology
Terre Haute, Indiana

Fast Facts About the Program	Fast Facts About the School
• **Established:** 1968 • **Enrollment:** 100 • **Faculty:** 24 (19 FT, 5 PT) • **Student/Faculty Ratio:** 4:1 • **Degrees Conferred Since Inception:** 500 • **Degrees Conferred in 1991:** 21 • **Contact:** Professor William A. Dando, Chairperson, Department of Geography and Geology, Indiana State University, Terre Haute, IN 47809; phone 812-237-2444	• State-supported coed university • 91-acre campus in urban setting • **Enrollment:** 11,783 • **Faculty:** 814 • **Tuition:** State resident: $2272; nonresident: $5490 • **Room and Board:** $3211 • **Application Deadline:** 8/15 • **Entrance Difficulty Level:** Moderately difficult • **Contact:** Richard Riel, Assistant Vice-President for Academic Affairs/Director of Admissions, 812-237-2121

The Program

Majoring in either geography or geology leads to a Bachelor of Science or a Bachelor of Arts degree. The geography major requires a total of 50 credit hours. The core consists of 26 credit hours of classes such as physical environment, cartography, cultural geography, and remote sensing. The remaining 24 credit hours constitute a specialization tailored to the student's interests. The geology major requires 71 credit hours with 34 credit hours in such core subjects as field geology, paleontology, sedimentology and stratigraphy, and geomorphology. Another 6 credit hours from elective courses are required. Other requirements include 31 credit hours in physics, chemistry, and mathematics.

MAJORS
Geography
Geology

Special Features

Ongoing research associated with the graduate program has helped the department maintain a high-quality undergraduate program with a low student-instructor ratio. The department is well equipped with remote sensing, geographic information systems (GIS), climatology, cartography, hydrology, geomorphology, and petrology laboratories, as well as excellent teaching collections and a map library with over 250,000 items. An astronomy observatory is available for use by geology and geography students. Field studies are an important component of the program.

The Result

Employment opportunities for geographers include industrial development, location research, water and nature research, environmental and urban planning, remote sensing, and cartography; for geologists, opportunities are available in the petroleum and mining industries, government surveys, local governments, and environmental consulting firms.

Who's Recruiting Who on Campus

Employers (Positions): American Society of Agronomy (Soil and Groundwater Scientists); American Society of Consulting Planners (Environmental Planners); Bureau of Land Management (Land-Use Planners); Defense Mapping Agency (Cartographers); Environmental Defense Fund (Environmental Planners); U.S. Fish and Wildlife Service (Hydrologists)

LAMAR UNIVERSITY–BEAUMONT
Environmental Science
Beaumont, Texas

Fast Facts About the Program
- **Established:** 1968
- **Enrollment:** 92
- **Faculty:** 41 (40 FT, 1 PT)
- **Student/Faculty Ratio:** 2:1
- **Degrees Conferred Since Inception:** 79
- **Degrees Conferred in 1991:** 6
- **Contact:** Richard C. Harrel, Professor of Biology, Lamar University-Beaumont, Beaumont, TX 77710; phone 409-880-8255

Fast Facts About the School
- State-supported coed university
- 200-acre campus in urban setting
- **Enrollment:** 11,848
- **Faculty:** 725
- **Student/Faculty Ratio:** 24:1
- **Tuition:** State resident: $720; nonresident: $4860
- **Fees:** $654
- **Room and Board:** $2600
- **Application Deadline:** 8/1
- **Entrance Difficulty Level:** Minimally difficult
- **Contact:** James Rush, Director, Academic Services, 409-880-8354

The Program
The Environmental Science Program is interdisciplinary and emphasizes a broad understanding of ecological, industrial, and governmental concerns about the environment. The degree combines study in biology, chemistry, engineering, geology, and political science to prepare students for careers in numerous areas of environmental science, including regulatory agencies, industry, and consulting firms. The degree requires 133 to 136 semester hours, including a supervised internship.

MAJOR/CONCENTRATIONS
Environmental Science
Biology
Chemistry

Special Features
Facilities supporting the program include the Gulf Coast Hazardous Substance Research Center and the Environmental Chemistry Laboratory. Both are located on the Lamar University campus. Other facilities include a coastal and marine studies field station, located on Pleasure Island in Port Arthur, Texas, which houses classrooms, laboratories, and boats, and the Dujay Sanctuary, a 40-acre wooded tract located 35 miles north of campus next to the Big Thicket National Preserve.

The Result
Graduates of the program are employed by the Texas Water Commission; the Texas Air Control Board; the Texas Parks and Wildlife Department; the U.S. Environmental Protection Agency; the Department of the Interior; the U.S. Army Corps of Engineers; the U.S. Fish and Wildlife Service; and several city and county environmental agencies, river authorities, consulting firms, and industries. About 98% of graduates find employment in their field or enter graduate school within 6 months of graduation.

Who's Recruiting Who on Campus
Employers (Positions): Texas Water Commission (Field Investigators, Biologist/Environmental Quality Specialists, Petroleum Storage Tank Investigators, Wastewater Enforcement Coordinators); Texas Air Control Board (Field Investigators)

LIVINGSTON UNIVERSITY
Environmental Science
Livingston, Alabama

Fast Facts About the Program	Fast Facts About the School
• **Established:** 1984 • **Enrollment:** 45 • **Faculty:** 8 (all FT) • **Student/Faculty Ratio:** 6:1 • **Degrees Conferred Since Inception:** 40 • **Degrees Conferred in 1991:** 12 • **Contact:** Richard L. Buckner, Program Coordinator, Division of Natural Sciences and Mathematics, Livingston University, Livingston, AL 35470; phone 205-652-9661 Ext. 203	• State-supported comprehensive coed institution • 595-acre campus in small-town setting • **Enrollment:** 2,086 • **Faculty:** 110 • **Student/Faculty Ratio:** 18:1 • **Tuition:** $1440 • **Fees:** $219 • **Room and Board:** $2253 • **Application Deadline:** Rolling • **Entrance Difficulty Level:** Minimally difficult • **Contact:** Dr. Ervin L. Wood, Vice-President for Student Services, 205-652-9661 Ext. 352

The Program

The environmental science major provides basic knowledge in a wide variety of environmentally related fields, ranging from those with a physical science emphasis to those with a biological science

MAJOR
Environmental Science

emphasis. It is an 86-quarter-hour interdisciplinary major integrating biology, chemistry, computer science, geology, and physics. The student develops skills in the use of scientific instrumentation and the collection and interpretation of data. The curriculum provides the student with an understanding of the processes and principles that govern living systems and influence the environment and how human interactions can affect them.

Special Features

The last quarter of the Environmental Science Program is an 8-week internship. The student may intern at one of several sites, such as a major waste disposal firm, a regional environmental health department, paper mills, testing laboratories, and international chemical companies.The internship provides the student with 8 to 9 weeks of hands-on experience in environmentally related activities. This is particularly beneficial to the student when entering the job market.

The Result

Students may qualify for the state job of environmentalist or pollution control specialist or another comparable job in industry. The effectiveness of the program is demonstrated by the fact that 90% of graduates have found employment in their field or have enrolled in graduate school within 6 months of graduation.

Who's Recruiting Who on Campus

Employers: power companies, waste disposal companies, state health departments, environmental consulting firms, federal government agencies, chemical industry

LONG ISLAND UNIVERSITY, SOUTHAMPTON CAMPUS

Environmental Science
Southampton, New York

Fast Facts About the Program
- **Established:** 1981
- **Enrollment:** 54
- **Faculty:** 24 (20 FT, 4 PT)
- **Student/Faculty Ratio:** 2:1
- **Degrees Conferred Since Inception:** 18
- **Degrees Conferred in 1991:** 7
- **Contact:** Carol Gilbert, Director of Admissions, 208 M, Long Island University, Southampton Campus, 239 Montauk Highway, Southampton, NY 11968; phone 516-283-4000

Fast Facts About the School
- Independent comprehensive coed institution
- 110-acre campus in rural setting
- **Enrollment:** 1,458
- **Faculty:** 120
- **Student/Faculty Ratio:** 18:1
- **Tuition:** $9540
- **Fees:** $510
- **Room and Board:** $5060
- **Application Deadline:** Rolling
- **Entrance Difficulty Level:** Moderately difficult
- **Contact:** Carol Gilbert, Director of Admissions, 516-283-4000 Ext. 200

The Program
The objectives of the Environmental Science Program are to promote the interdisciplinary and disciplinary knowledge, skills, and techniques required to investigate environmental problems; produce graduates who have competence in an environmentally related area by providing a solid background in

MAJOR/CONCENTRATIONS
Environmental Science
Environmental Biology
Environmental Chemistry
Environmental Geology

one of 3 major discipline areas (biology, chemistry, and geology); and develop a sufficiently broad perspective and insight into related disciplines, which enable students to assess the condition of the environment and to participate effectively in the solution of environmental problems. Full-semester internships provide students with off-campus work experiences. In the junior or senior year, students may work full-time on projects that are related to their field. The National Wildlife Federation in Washington, D.C., and the Brookhaven National Laboratory on Long Island have LIU environmental science majors working on environmental projects on a regular basis. Long Island University also offers a program in environmental studies.

Special Features
Special features of the program include an on-campus marine station, an aquaculture lab, and a varied local ecology that includes both freshwater and saltwater environments. Co-op opportunities are also available.

The Result
Approximately 93% of graduates find employment in their field and/or start advanced programs within 6 months of graduation. Recent graduates are currently employed in environmental positions with the National Park Service and Brookhaven Laboratory, environmental education with the Group for the South Fork (conservation), and aquaculture with the National Marine Fisheries Service.

LOUISIANA STATE UNIVERSITY AND AGRICULTURAL AND MECHANICAL COLLEGE
Environmental Management Systems
Baton Rouge, Louisiana

Fast Facts About the Program
- **Established:** 1988
- **Enrollment:** 129
- **Degrees Conferred Since Inception:** 24
- **Degrees Conferred in 1991:** 8
- **Contact:** Dr. Sam Feagley, Associate Professor, Agronomy Department, Louisiana State University and Agricultural and Mechanical College, Baton Rouge, LA 70803; phone 504-388-2110

Fast Facts About the School
- State-supported coed university
- 1,944-acre campus in urban setting
- **Enrollment:** 26,138
- **Faculty:** 1,348
- **Student/Faculty Ratio:** 19:1
- **Tuition:** State resident: $2058; nonresident: $5258
- **Room and Board:** $2710
- **Application Deadline:** 7/1
- **Entrance Difficulty Level:** Moderately difficult
- **Contact:** Lisa Harris, Director of Admissions, 504-388-1175

The Program
The goal of this degree program is to prepare students for work involving the improvement of the quality of the air, water, and land and soil. The program requires that students complete 134 credit hours in order to graduate and have a strong background in basic sciences (biology/microbiology, chemistry, and math) and applied sciences (environmental science, geography, geology, soil science, and oceanography and coastal science). The program was initiated in 1988 and is growing rapidly.

> **MAJOR/CONCENTRATIONS**
> **Environmental Management Systems**
> Air Quality
> Land/Soil Quality
> Water Quality

Special Features
Numerous student jobs are available with faculty members conducting environmental research. Students are encouraged to interact with these scientists and receive training they would not get in the classroom. A student organization has been established, which meets on a regular basis with invited speakers. Students have also formed a club to work on environment-related projects.

The Result
The majority of students are working for engineering and environmental consulting firms and state agencies such as Natural Resources and Environmental Quality. Examples of job titles include scientist, environmental quality specialist, site operator, and lab technician. Several students are going to graduate school to study applied sciences, such as environmental science and soil environmental chemistry.

Who's Recruiting Who on Campus
Employers: Dames and Moore, CH2M HILL, Radian Corporation, CK and Associates, Department of Environmental Quality, Department of Natural Resources

---

MARIST COLLEGE
Environmental Science
Poughkeepsie, New York

Fast Facts About the Program
- **Established:** 1979
- **Enrollment:** 64
- **Faculty:** 6 (4 FT, 2 PT)
- **Student/Faculty Ratio:** 11:1
- **Degrees Conferred Since Inception:** 76
- **Degrees Conferred in 1991:** 3
- **Contact:** Dr. Thomas Lynch, Director of Environmental Science, Marist College, Poughkeepsie, NY 12601; phone 914-575-3000 Ext. 2443

Fast Facts About the School
- Independent comprehensive coed institution
- 120-acre campus in small-town setting
- **Enrollment:** 4,274
- **Faculty:** 345
- **Student/Faculty Ratio:** 19:1
- **Tuition:** $8970
- **Room and Board:** $5210
- **Application Deadline:** 3/1
- **Entrance Difficulty Level:** Moderately difficult
- **Contact:** Harry W. Wood, Vice-President for Admissions and Enrollment Planning, 914-575-3000 Ext. 2227

The Program
The Environmental Science Program leads to the Bachelor of Science degree. The 120-credit-hour curriculum gives students the knowledge, skills, and abilities necessary to comprehend current environmental problems and their scientific solutions in the context of ethical, economic, political, and legal

> **MAJOR/CONCENTRATIONS**
> **Environmental Science**
> Biology
> Chemistry
> Public Policy

constraints. The student is broadly trained in natural and social sciences, liberal arts, and oral and written communication. Specialization in 1 of 3 tracks provides the technical background needed to secure entry into graduate school or the job market. All students are required to complete a 6-credit internship.

Special Features
The campus provides an ideal setting for environmental study. Located nearby are the Vanderbilt and Roosevelt national historic sites, several state parks, and the Cary Arboretum. Together these areas provide access to Hudson River frontage, numerous wetlands and streams, and thousands of acres of upland fields and forests. Students in the program have access to 11 laboratories and a large greenhouse in Donnelly Hall as well as the sophisticated computer-based geographic information systems laboratory. Students can complete their junior year at a foreign institution through participation in the Marist Abroad Program. Internships and volunteer opportunities can be arranged with local government agencies, private consulting firms, and environmental advocacy groups.

The Result
Direct entry into the public or private work sector represents the option most often followed by Marist graduates. Recent graduates are working in a variety of settings, including as director of an environmental testing laboratory, as a recycling specialist, and as environmental scientists for major computer and environmental consulting firms. The areas of waste-site remediation, air- and water-quality monitoring, environmental assessment, and resource recovery offer excellent job opportunitites. Seventy-five percent of graduates find employment in their field or enroll in graduate school within 6 months of graduation.

NEW ENGLAND COLLEGE
Environmental Science
Henniker, New Hampshire

Fast Facts About the Program
- **Established:** 1975
- **Enrollment:** 30
- **Faculty:** 9 (8 FT, 1 PT)
- **Student/Faculty Ratio:** 3:1
- **Degrees Conferred Since Inception:** 165
- **Degrees Conferred in 1991:** 2
- **Contact:** Dr. Debbie Eustis-Grandy, Assistant Professor of Environmental Science, New England College, 8 Depot Hill Road, Henniker, NH 03242-3293; phone 603-428-2368

Fast Facts About the School
- Independent comprehensive coed institution
- 212-acre campus in a rural setting
- **Enrollment:** 1,030
- **Faculty:** 117
- **Student/Faculty Ratio:** 14:1
- **Tuition:** $11,990
- **Room and Board:** $4970
- **Application Deadline:** Rolling
- **Entrance Difficulty Level:** Minimally difficult
- **Contact:** John Spaulding, Director of Admissions, 603-428-2223

The Program

The purpose of the Environmental Science Program is to prepare students for career options in environmental biology, environmental chemistry, environmental geology, ecology, toxicology, and environmental health. Graduates of the program

MAJOR/CONCENTRATION

Environmental Science
Environmental Studies

are actively involved in a number of environmentally related fields. This program, which began in 1975, was modified in 1990 to focus more on scientific principles and includes an internship/independent study requirement. Students complete 65 credit hours covering courses in biology, chemistry, geology, and environmental sciences. Continuing students are eligible for the Bagley Scholarship, given to outstanding students majoring in the sciences (biology, engineering, environmental science).

Special Features

A variety of special facilities and resources are available at NEC and are used extensively for both teaching and student research. These facilities include greenhouses, an environmental growth chamber, approximately 150 acres of natural areas located adjacent to the science building, and Williams Island—an island off the coast of eastern Maine that serves as a biological research site. New England College also has a campus in England to which students are encouraged to go for at least one semester or summer session.

The Result

Most graduates of NEC's program enter the work force after graduation. Eighty percent of graduates find employment or enroll in graduate school within 6 months of graduation. Placement is most often in private consulting firms, or in federal, state, or local governments.

NORTHERN ARIZONA UNIVERSITY
Environmental Sciences
Flagstaff, Arizona

Fast Facts About the Program
- **Established:** 1972
- **Enrollment:** 170
- **Faculty:** 13 (12 FT, 1 PT)
- **Student/Faculty Ratio:** 13:1
- **Degrees Conferred Since Inception:** 400
- **Degrees Conferred in 1991:** 28
- **Contact:** Ernest S. Gladney, Director of Environmental Sciences Program, P.O. Box 5694, Northern Arizona University, Flagstaff, AZ 86011-5694; phone 602-523-9333

Fast Facts About the School
- State-supported coed university
- 730-acre campus in small-town setting
- **Enrollment:** 17,698
- **Faculty:** 927
- **Tuition:** State resident: $1590; nonresident: $6242
- **Room and Board:** $2776
- **Application Deadline:** 7/15
- **Entrance Difficulty Level:** Moderately difficult
- **Contact:** Molly Carder, Director of Admissions, 602-523-5511

The Program
The program consists of 8 required courses in the environmental sciences core and a minimum of 31 hours in one of the 7 fields of emphasis (credit requirements vary with discipline selected). Students are encouraged to broaden their knowledge in related fields by choosing environmentally focused electives offered in concentration fields as well as in forestry, political science, and technology. The Lisa Marie Jones Memorial Scholarship in the Environmental Sciences, with $250 and $500 awards, is available to juniors and seniors.

MAJOR/CONCENTRATIONS
Environmental Sciences
Applied Geology
Applied Mathematics
Biology
Chemistry
Engineering
Environmental Management
Microbiology

Special Features
On-campus facilities for the program include the U.S. Forest Service Rocky Mountain Range and Experiment Station, a National Park Service cooperative unit, the Bilby Research Center, the Grand Canyon Trust, and the Transition Zone Horticultural Institute. A variety of other facilities within a 100-mile radius of Flagstaff include the Museum of Northern Arizona, Lowell Observatory, the U.S. Naval Observatory, the U.S. Geological Survey Field Center, the Grand Canyon National Park, and Petrified Forest National Park.

The Result
Approximately 50% of program graduates go directly into graduate school. Those who elect to accept employment take positions with private industry, government laboratories and agencies, consulting firms, and public utilities. Virtually all majors in the program find a job in their field or go on to graduate study within 6 months of graduation.

Who's Recruiting Who on Campus
Employers: Los Alamos National Laboratory, Lawrence Livermore National Laboratory, Idaho National Engineering Laboratory, Arizona Public Service, Salt River Project, Southern California Electric, DOW Chemical, Stone Container, Peabody Coal Co., and state and local governments

RUTGERS, THE STATE UNIVERSITY OF NEW JERSEY, COOK COLLEGE

Environmental Sciences

New Brunswick, New Jersey

Fast Facts About the Program

- **Established:** 1973
- **Enrollment:** 350
- **Faculty:** 21 (15 FT, 6 PT)
- **Student/Faculty Ratio:** 17:1
- **Degrees Conferred Since Inception:** 1,138
- **Degrees Conferred in 1991:** 80
- **Contact:** Dr. Samuel D. Faust, Department of Environmental Sciences, P.O. Box 231, Rutgers, The State University of New Jersey, Cook College, New Brunswick, NJ 08903; phone 908-932-8013

Fast Facts About the School

- State-supported 4-year coed college
- 2,686-acre campus in small-town setting
- **Enrollment:** 2,874
- **Faculty:** 90
- **Student/Faculty Ratio:** 16:1
- **Tuition:** State resident: $3456; nonresident: $7032
- **Fees:** $710
- **Room and Board:** $4018
- **Application Deadline:** 1/15
- **Entrance Difficulty Level:** Moderately difficult
- **Contact:** Dr. Elizabeth Mitchell, Assistant Vice President for University Undergraduate Admissions, 908-932-3770

The Program

The curriculum of the environmental sciences undergraduate program provides a foundation for the application of basic sciences to the evaluation and solution of environmental problems. Students achieve a broad understanding of the complexity of environmental interactions and acquire a detailed understanding of one aspect of the environmental science discipline by taking 1 of 9 options. Cook College also offers a program in environmental and business economics.

MAJOR/CONCENTRATIONS

Environmental Sciences
Environmental Chemistry
Environmental Health Sciences
Environmental Teacher Education
Industrial Hygiene and Safety
Pollution and Treatment Sciences
Preparation for Marine Studies
Radiation-Nuclear Sciences
Soil Science
Water Resources

Special Features

In the cooperative education program, each student has a faculty sponsor and is required to write a learning contract, a final report, and an oral presentation if a letter grade is requested. Typical placements are with the New Jersey Department of Environmental Protection, federal EPA, and various industries in New Jersey.

The Result

Ninety-five percent of graduates find employment or enroll in graduate school within 6 months of graduation. In recent years, a significant number of graduates (47%) were employed by the private sector. About 20% were employed in the public sector (including environmental health and general environmental jobs). About 18% of graduates go directly into professional school and many fully employed students are enrolled in part-time graduate programs. Fifty percent of graduates are employed in New Jersey.

SAINT MARY'S COLLEGE OF MINNESOTA
Environmental Biology
Winona, Minnesota

Fast Facts About the Program
- **Established:** 1976
- **Enrollment:** 16
- **Faculty:** 12 (all FT)
- **Student/Faculty Ratio:** 1:1
- **Degrees Conferred Since Inception:** 100
- **Degrees Conferred in 1991:** 9
- **Contact:** Dr. Clare Karte, Chair, Biology Department, Saint Mary's College of Minnesota, 700 Terrace Heights, Winona, MN 55987-1399; phone 507-457-1543

Fast Facts About the School
- Independent Roman Catholic comprehensive coed institution
- 400-acre campus in small-town setting
- **Enrollment:** 3,800
- **Faculty:** 128
- **Student/Faculty Ratio:** 11:1
- **Tuition:** $9630
- **Fees:** $100
- **Room and Board:** $3250
- **Application Deadline:** Rolling
- **Entrance Difficulty Level:** Moderately difficult
- **Contact:** Anthony Piscitiello, Vice-President for Admission, 507-457-1700

The Program

SMC's environmental biology major is a science-based major that requires courses in chemistry, mathematics, and physics. Undergraduate research is a required component of the program, although in special circumstances an approved internship may be substituted. Environmental elective course

MAJOR/CONCENTRATIONS
Environmental Biology
Resource Management
Environmental Toxicology
Computer Applications in Ecology

offerings include ecological spatial data analysis, ecology of land use, environmental toxicology, fisheries biology, ornithology, and wildlife biology. Two U.S. Fish and Wildlife Service cooperative agreements provide special work opportunities.

Special Features

Environmental studies at SMC are enhanced by both the outdoor and indoor environments. The immediate surroundings of the college include the upper Mississippi River, with its backwater marshes and wooded sloughs; lakes; trout streams (one of which flows through campus); hardwood forests; goat prairies; agricultural land; and the Trempealeau National Wildlife Refuge, which includes over 4,000 acres of nearly pristine marsh and upland prairie habitat. The indoor environment is in Hoffman Hall, which is part of the Adducci Science Center. Laboratory facilities are modern and extremely well equipped for study. Field equipment is abundant and diverse. Toxicological equipment of special interest includes a capillary gas chromatograph, high-performance liquid chromatograph, and atomic absorption spectrophotometer as well as all the necessary support equipment.

The Result

The success of SMC biology and environmental biology majors has been documented repeatedly. In a 1986 survey taken by the Great Lakes Colleges Association that ranked schools on the number of graduates achieving doctorates. SMC ranked 43rd out of more than 1,500 institutions granting degrees in the life sciences. About 95% of graduates find employment in their field or enroll in graduate school within 6 months of graduation.

SHIPPENSBURG UNIVERSITY OF PENNSYLVANIA

Geoenvironmental Studies
Shippensburg, Pennsylvania

Fast Facts About the Program
- **Established:** 1970
- **Enrollment:** 175
- **Faculty:** 14 (13 FT, 1 PT)
- **Student/Faculty Ratio:** 13:1
- **Degrees Conferred Since Inception:** 508
- **Degrees Conferred in 1991:** 46
- **Contact:** Dr. John E. Benhart, Chair, Department of Geography–Earth Science, Shippensburg University, Shippensburg, PA 17257; phone 717-532-1685

Fast Facts About the School
- State-supported comprehensive coed institution
- 200-acre campus in rural setting
- **Enrollment:** 6,696
- **Faculty:** 358
- **Student/Faculty Ratio:** 20:1
- **Tuition:** State resident: $2628; nonresident: $4892
- **Fees:** $480
- **Room and Board:** $2796
- **Application Deadline:** Rolling
- **Entrance Difficulty Level:** Moderately difficult
- **Contact:** Doyle Bickers, Dean of Admissions, 771-532-1231

The Program
The Department of Geography–Earth Sciences offers undergraduate programs leading to the Bachelor of Arts and the Bachelor of Science in Education. The undergraduate programs are

MAJOR
Geoenvironmental Studies

designed to give students an appreciation of the physical and cultural environment of the earth. Students develop skills in collecting, recording, and interpreting geoenvironmental data. They become involved in laboratory work, field investigations, and environmental management, all of which sharpen their skills to arrive at solutions based on an inductive application of all available sources and materials. Students identify and distinguish trends and analyze and interpret physical, socioeconomic, and geopolitical patterns in an urban, rural, or regional setting. The fundamental geographic themes of location, place, interrelationships between the physical and cultural environment, movement, and regions are emphasized. The department's object of analysis is the earth's surface and its purpose, understanding how that surface is structured and differentiated, and how people have affected the landscape.

Special Features
The department has a strong interdisciplinary nature. With diverse backgrounds, departmental faculty integrate findings from a variety of fields to develop insights on real problems in various areas, such as studying environmental hazards in the Cumberland Valley or environmental conservation issues in Salzburg, Austria. In departmental courses and programs, faculty explain that location is important, that there are reasons areas and places are different physically and culturally, and that knowledge of how territory is organized and changed is a key issue in science and society.

The Result
Eighty-five percent of graduates of the Geoenvironmental Studies program find jobs or advance to graduate study within 6 months of completion of the program.

STATE UNIVERSITY OF NEW YORK COLLEGE AT PLATTSBURGH

Environmental Science
Plattsburgh, New York

Fast Facts About the Program
- **Established:** 1974
- **Enrollment:** 211
- **Faculty:** 17 (14 FT, 3 PT)
- **Student/Faculty Ratio:** 12:1
- **Degrees Conferred Since Inception:** 900
- **Degrees Conferred in 1991:** 35
- **Contact:** Dr. Malcolm Fairweather, Director, Center for Earth and Environmental Science, State University of New York College at Plattsburgh, Plattsburgh, NY 12901; phone 518-564-2028

Fast Facts About the School
- State-supported comprehensive coed institution
- 265-acre campus in small-town setting
- **Enrollment:** 6,344
- **Faculty:** 368
- **Tuition:** State resident: $2150; nonresident: $5750
- **Fees:** $215
- **Room and Board:** $3642
- **Application Deadline:** Rolling
- **Entrance Difficulty Level:** Moderately difficult
- **Contact:** Richard Higgins, Director of Admissions, 518-564-2040

The Program

Students in the environmental science major take part in a broad interdisciplinary program. In the junior and senior years, students study the ecological, physical, and human areas of the discipline and take one technical skills course plus environmental electives. Four scholarships, valued at $2000 each, are awarded to students in environmental science. For the geology major, there is a study option in environmental geology that builds upon a traditional core of geology courses. The emphasis of this applied program is to integrate both the physical and the biological aspects of environmental science with geology.

> **MAJORS/CONCENTRATIONS**
> **Environmental Science**
> Environmental Systems
> Natural Resources Planning and Management
> **Geology**
> Environmental Geology

Special Features

Each fall the Center for Earth and Environmental Science conducts the Applied Environmental Semester at the W. H. Miner Agricultural Research Institute. Each class occupies a full day, is taught by regular center faculty, and makes full use of the 6,800-acre facility. Study-abroad programs are available with major institutions in Canada, England, and Mexico. The most popular exchange program is with the University of East Anglia's Centre for Environmental Studies in England. A wide variety of internships are conducted each year.

The Result

Positions as environmental scientists, laboratory/field technicians, research analysts, and project managers are found with environmental consulting firms, the New York State Department of Environmental Conservation, the Fish and Wildlife Service, and waste management agencies. Seventy percent of graduates find employment or enroll in graduate school within 6 months of graduation. Students continuing their education are attending Pace University Law School, New Jersey Institute of Technology, University of Rhode Island, Harvard School of Design, and University of Vermont.

SUSQUEHANNA UNIVERSITY
Department of Geological and Environmental Science
Selinsgrove, Pennsylvania

Fast Facts About the Program
- **Established:** 1986
- **Enrollment:** 38
- **Faculty:** 3 (all FT)
- **Student/Faculty Ratio:** 13:1
- **Degrees Conferred Since Inception:** 15
- **Degrees Conferred in 1991:** 4
- **Contact:** Dr. Richard H. Lowright, Associate Professor, Department of Geological and Environmental Science, Susquehanna University, Selingsgrove, PA 17870; phone 717-372-4216

Fast Facts About the School
- Independent 4-year coed college, affiliated with Lutheran Church
- 190-acre campus in small-town setting
- **Enrollment:** 1,433
- **Faculty:** 137
- **Student/Faculty Ratio:** 14:1
- **Tuition:** $14,510
- **Fees:** $270
- **Room and Board:** $4200
- **Application Deadline:** 3/15
- **Entrance Difficulty Level:** Moderately difficult
- **Contact:** Richard Ziegler, Director of Admissions, 717-372-4260

The Program
The Institute for Environmental Studies was founded in 1973, and in 1986 merged with the Department of Geological Sciences and was renamed the Department of Geological and Environmental Sciences. The program focuses on environmental aspects of air, land, and water and has three chief goals. They are to foster an understanding of the earth's environmental systems and the interelationships between humans and the environment; to prepare the professional scientists who will put to practical use the environmental principles and methodologies for the advancement of human knowledge and the good of society; and to conduct research that is directed toward increasing an understanding of the relationship between humans and the earth's environment. The program leads to a Bachelor of Arts in environmental science degree, which requires 40 semester hours of major courses.

> **MAJOR/CONCENTRATIONS**
> **Environmental Science**
> Air Quality
> Hydrogeology
> Water Quality

Special Features
The field component of the program is supported by a hydrogeologic field laboratory, where instruction in, and research on, groundwater flow and contamination are carried out. Additional environmental instruction takes place at the University's Hepner Field Station. Internships with state and federal agencies are available to juniors and seniors and are limited to one semester each. The department's Visiting Scientist Program brings students into contact with environmental professionals.

The Result
The typical graduate is employed by environmental consulting firms or a state environmental regulatory agency. Positions include work as hydrogeologists, environmental specialists, and geologic technicians. Graduate studies are pursued in resource management, groundwater hydrology, and wetlands among others. Eighty-five percent of graduates find employment or enroll in graduate school within 6 months of graduation.

TROY STATE UNIVERSITY
Environmental Science
Troy, Alabama

Fast Facts About the Program
- **Established:** 1976
- **Enrollment:** 47
- **Faculty:** 18 (15 FT, 3 PT)
- **Student/Faculty Ratio:** 3:1
- **Degrees Conferred Since Inception:** 60
- **Degrees Conferred in 1991:** 3
- **Environmental Library Holdings:** 1,000 bound volumes; 30 periodical subscriptions; 600 records/tapes/CDs
- **Contact:** Charles P. Chapman, Chairman, Biology Department, 107 McCall Hall, Troy State University, Troy, AL 36082; phone 205-670-3401 or 205-670-3581

Fast Facts About the School
- State-supported comprehensive coed institution
- 500-acre campus in small-town setting
- **Enrollment:** 4,350
- **Faculty:** 205
- **Student/Faculty Ratio:** 30:1
- **Tuition:** State resident: $1287; nonresident: $1887
- **Fees:** $300
- **Room and Board:** $2325
- **Application Deadline:** Rolling
- **Entrance Difficulty Level:** Moderately difficult
- **Contact:** Jim Hutto, Dean of Enrollment Services, 205-670-3179

The Program
The Environmental Science Program is interdisciplinary, requiring course work in biological, physical, and social sciences. It requires 180 quarter hours for a Bachelor of Science degree.

MAJOR
Environmental Science

Special Features
The Troy State Arboretum, located adjacent to campus, includes 75 acres of woodland, nature trails, a pond, and wetland areas. It has a diversity of plants and animals and is used by the Environmental Science Program to support and expand classroom activities. The Pocosin Reserve, 18 acres of treasure forest located 6 miles east of Troy, is one of the few remaining parts of the upland swamp that has not been altered by cultivation. It is available to students and scholars studying the environment with emphasis on preserving the rare flora and fauna unique to the Pocosin. The Environmental Education Certification Program (Class-B Certification) is the only one in the state of Alabama. Recently, Troy State University appointed Dr. James Gore as an Eminent Scholar in Environmental Science.

The Result
Ninety percent of graduates find employment or enroll in graduate school within 6 months of graduation.

Who's Recruiting Who on Campus
Employers: Alabama Department of Public Health and Department of Environmental Management, Georgia Department of Public Health and Department of Environmental Health, Alabama Power Company, U.S. Department of Environmental Protection, Waste Disposal Corporation. **Positions:** Environmental Protection Specialist, Environmental Technician, Public Health Environmentalist.

UNIVERSITY OF CALIFORNIA, DAVIS
Environmental Biology and Management
Davis, California

Fast Facts About the Program	Fast Facts About the School
• **Established:** 1978	• State-supported coed university
• **Enrollment:** 180	• 6,010-acre campus in suburban setting
• **Faculty:** 26 (25 FT, 1 PT)	• **Enrollment:** 23,302
• **Student/Faculty Ratio:** 7:1	• **Faculty:** 1,626
• **Degrees Conferred Since Inception:** 200	• **Student/Faculty Ratio:** 19:1
• **Degrees Conferred in 1991:** 30	• **Tuition:** State resident: $0; nonresident: $10,677
• **Contact:** Delores Dument, Staff Adviser, Division of Environmental Studies, University of California-Davis, Davis, CA 95616; phone 916-752-3088	• **Fees:** $2979
	• **Room and Board:** $5820
	• **Application Deadline:** 11/30
	• **Entrance Difficulty Level:** Very difficult
	• **Contact:** Dr. Gary Tudor, Director of Admissions, 916-752-2971

The Program
The Environmental Biology and Management program is a natural science program that emphasizes ecology and environmental processes combined with an introduction to the social science disciplines and analytical tools used in environmental decision making. Students may specialize in either environmental biology or environmental management.

MAJOR/CONCENTRATIONS

Environmental Biology and Management
Environmental Biology
Environmental Management

Special Features
UC-Davis, has the following campus facilities and field stations for students of environmental science and policy: California Agricultural Experiment Station, Institute of Ecology, Institute of Toxicology and Health, Tucker Herbarium, Jepson Prairie Reserve, Putah Creek Campus Reserve, Bodega Marine Laboratory, Water Resource Center, and Stebbons Cold Canyon Reserve. Students in the Sustainable Agriculture Program use the Student Experimental Farm.

The Result
Graduates of the program typically pursue advanced degrees in biological sciences, environmental law, and public administration. Seventy-five percent of graduates find employment or enroll in graduate school within 6 months of graduation. UC-Davis sponsors campuswide workshops and job fairs for students pursuing environmental careers. State and regional governments recruit for departments of natural resources.

UNIVERSITY OF CALIFORNIA, RIVERSIDE
Environmental Sciences
Riverside, California

Fast Facts About the Program
- **Established:** 1971
- **Enrollment:** 120
- **Faculty:** 12 (all FT)
- **Student/Faculty Ratio:** 10:1
- **Degrees Conferred Since Inception:** 400
- **Degrees Conferred in 1991:** 30
- **Environmental Library Holdings:** 250 bound volumes; 150 titles on microform; 5 periodical subscriptions; 15 records/tapes/CDs
- **Contact:** Peter Diage, Assistant Chair, Environmental Sciences, University of California, Riverside, Riverside, CA 92521; phone 714-787-3850

Fast Facts About the School
- State-supported coed university
- 1,200-acre campus in suburban setting
- **Enrollment:** 8,890
- **Faculty:** 718
- **Student/Faculty Ratio:** 14:1
- **Tuition:** State resident: $0; nonresident: $7701
- **Fees:** $2373
- **Room and Board:** $5360
- **Application Deadline:** 11/30
- **Entrance Difficulty Level:** Very difficult
- **Contact:** Marion McCarthy, Associate Admissions Officer, 714-787-3411

The Program
For over 20 years, UC Riverside's Environmental Sciences Program has provided an interdisciplinary curriculum designed to meet the educational needs of those interested in solving environmental problems. All majors are required to take courses in biology, chemistry, calculus, English, economics, government, statistics, and computer science, as well as in soil science, water science, air science, environmental economics, environmental management, and environmental impact analysis.

MAJOR/CONCENTRATIONS
Environmental Sciences
  Environmental Toxicology
  Natural Sciences
  Social Sciences
  Soil Science

Special Features
Special facilities on campus include the department's research labs, the California Statewide Air Pollution Research Center, and the university system's Natural Lands Reserve System. Cooperative research arrangements are conducted with the U.S. Forest Service Forest Fire Research Laboratory, U.S. Department of Agriculture Salinity Laboratory, California Regional Water Quality Control Board, and South Coast Air Quality Management District. Students interact with members of the government and business community through the Environmental Internship Program. International exchange of students is facilitated through the University of California System's Education Abroad Program.

The Result
Program graduates have successfully completed advanced training in almost every scientific discipline as well as in professional schools of medicine, law, engineering, and education. Alumni currently hold positions with the U.S. Environmental Protection Agency, the U.S. Bureau of Land Management, and various state and local agencies. More commonly, they are employed by private businesses. Woodward Clyde Consultants, General Dynamics, and various energy, manufacturing, and consulting firms are among the private businesses that have hired graduates.

UNIVERSITY OF DENVER
Environmental Science
Denver, Colorado

Fast Facts About the Program
- **Established:** 1973
- **Enrollment:** 65
- **Faculty:** 10 (8 FT, 2 PT)
- **Student/Faculty Ratio:** 7:1
- **Degrees Conferred Since Inception:** 100
- **Degrees Conferred in 1991:** 12
- **Contact:** Michael W. Monahan/Donald R. Sullivan, Co-directors of Environmental Science Program, University of Denver, Denver, CO 80208; phone 303-871-3540

Fast Facts About the School
- Independent coed university
- 125-acre campus in urban setting
- **Enrollment:** 8,019
- **Faculty:** 395
- **Student/Faculty Ratio:** 13:1
- **Tuition:** $13,572
- **Fees:** $148
- **Room and Board:** $4306
- **Application Deadline:** Rolling
- **Entrance Difficulty Level:** Moderately difficult
- **Contact:** Susan Hunt, Director of Admission Counseling, 303-871-2036

The Program

The Environmental Science Program offers two degree options. The B.S. in environmental science is designed to build a solid foundation in the natural sciences, while preparing students for problem-solving skills in technical areas of air, water, and soil

> **MAJORS**
>
> B.S. in Environmental Science
> B.A. in Environmental Science

pollution. The B.A. in environmental science seeks to develop the scientific understanding of environmental science, while offering maximum flexibility to students in balancing technical and social solutions to environmental questions.

Special Features

The Colorado Front Range offers an exceptional learning environment. The campus is just an hour's drive to habitats ranging from prairie to conifer forests and Alpine tundra. Courses offer many half-day field trips off campus and extended travel to field locations. Junior-Senior Seminar in Geography includes a 4-day field trip, which has investigated the oil-shale region of northwestern Colorado and the geography and geology of southwestern Colorado. Alpine ecology students spend a week at the University's mountain field station on Mt. Evans, while tropical ecology students cap their winter quarter of classroom lectures with a 10-day field trip over spring break to rain forest and coral reef ecology in Belize. Geography students have access to the Soils and Pollen Analysis Laboratory. Because Denver serves as the regional headquarters for various resource management agencies of the federal government, students have many potential opportunities for off-campus internships. Internships with state and municipal governments, corporations, and private organizations are also offered.

The Result

Within 6 months of graduation, 75% of students are employed in or seeking an advanced degree in the following areas: environmental law, corporate law, toxic-waste management, environmental consulting, urban planning, fish aquaculture, systems analysis, mined land reclamation, and regional recycling.

UNIVERSITY OF DUBUQUE
Environmental Science
Dubuque, Iowa

Fast Facts About the Program	Fast Facts About the School
• **Established:** 1980 • **Enrollment:** 21 • **Faculty:** 13 (11 FT, 2 PT) • **Student/Faculty Ratio:** 2:1 • **Degrees Conferred Since Inception:** 45 • **Degrees Conferred in 1991:** 5 • **Contact:** Dr. Robert M. Miller, Director of Environmental Science Programs, University of Dubuque, Dubuque, IA 52001; phone 319-589-3143	• Independent Presbyterian comprehensive coed institution • 56-acre campus in suburban setting • **Enrollment:** 1,200 • **Faculty:** 79 • **Student/Faculty Ratio:** 15:1 • **Tuition:** $9840 • **Room and Board:** $3365 • **Application Deadline:** 8/15 • **Entrance Difficulty Level:** Moderately difficult • **Contact:** Mitchell J. Pies, Dean for University Admissions, 319-589-3200

The Program

An interdisciplinary academic major in environmental science was organized in 1980, requiring students to complete a total of 60 credit hours. The major calls for the completion of courses in biology, chemistry, and geology. Required courses in ecology and environmental analysis focus the science base on the environment. An off-campus internship (junior year) with environmental professionals provides practical experience, while a required independent research project in the senior year allows the study of environmental problems. Field study features the Mississippi River, nearby forests and prairies, and trips to Florida and New Mexico.

MAJOR/CONCENTRATIONS

Environmental Science
  Biology
  Chemistry
  Geology

Special Features

On-campus facilities include a science hall housing laboratories equipped with both standard and advanced instrumentation such as an electron microscope and atomic absorption spectrophotometer used in environmental analysis. Portable sampling equipment for both water and air is used extensively in the field. Faculty members work closely with professionals from the Iowa Department of Natural Resources and the Four Mounds Foundation to provide students with relevant training while forums and seminars bring both public and private sector representatives to campus to interact with students.

Who's Recruiting Who on Campus

Employers (Positions): Aires Environmental (Asbestos Monitoring Technician); Iowa Department of Natural Resources (Fisheries and Wildlife Technician); Iowa-Illinois Thermal Insulation (Environmental Health Technician); Johnson County, Iowa (Roadside Vegetation Manager); Linn County, Iowa (Air Pollution Control Specialist); Lyon County, Iowa (Park Ranger/Naturalist); National Environmental Testing (Environmental Health Specialist); Quantum Chemical Company (Environmental Technician); Kansas Department of Health and Environment (Air Quality Specialist); Terracon Environmental (Environmental Scientist)

UNIVERSITY OF MISSISSIPPI
Freshwater Biology
Oxford, Mississippi

Fast Facts About the Program
- **Enrollment:** 200
- **Faculty:** 10 (all FT)
- **Student/Faculty Ratio:** 20:1
- **Degrees Conferred in 1991:** 80
- **Contact:** James Kushlan, Chair, Department of Biology, University of Mississippi, Oxford, MS 38077; phone 601-732-7203

Fast Facts About the School
- State-supported coed university
- 2,300-acre campus in small-town setting
- **Enrollment:** 11,033
- **Faculty:** 460
- **Tuition:** State resident: $2221; nonresident: $3683
- **Room and Board:** $2650
- **Application Deadline:** 7/31
- **Entrance Difficulty Level:** Moderately difficult
- **Contact:** Beckett Howorth, Director, Admissions and Records, 601-232-7226

The Program

At the University of Mississippi the importance placed on fresh water is reflected in its status as a central theme of research and study in the Department of Biology. The Freshwater Biology Program

MAJOR

Biological Sciences

offers a Bachelor of Arts or Bachelor of Science in Biological Sciences degree, provides training for both undergraduate and graduate students, and also serves as a center for research into fundamental and applied freshwater ecology. Among the areas of interest pursued by students in the program are water quality; evolutionary ecology; acoustics; ecology of ponds, lakes, and reservoirs; structure and function of wetlands; wetlands as transformers of agricultural chemicals; nutrient cycling; ecology and conservation of aquatic birds; responses of plants and animals to water management; effects of toxicants on aquatic systems and sediments; and sport fisheries research and aquaculture.

Special Features

The development of the Biological Field Station is one of the most promising and exciting aspects of the Freshwater Biology Program. Located 8 miles from campus, the 710-acre station encompasses over 140 regulated research ponds and wetlands, which vary in size from $\frac{1}{10}$ of an acre to $1\frac{1}{2}$ acres. Numerous springs provide exceptionally high quality water to all ponds year-round. The station has a full-time manager and staff, a fish hatchery building, artificial streams, and a wide diversity of aquatic and terrestrial habitats. The Research Institute of Pharmaceutical Sciences, the National Center for Physical Acoustics, and a modern on-campus computer department that houses a Cyber 205 supercomputer are evidence of the University's commitment to research. The Biology Department supports an aquarium laboratory, an animal care facility, and the University of Mississippi Biology Museum.

The Result

Graduates enter such fields as food production, sanitation, pollution control, environmental management, horticulture, and environmental consulting. Nearly all graduates find employment in their field or go on to advanced studies within 6 months of graduation.

UNIVERSITY OF MISSOURI–COLUMBIA
Agronomy
Columbia, Missouri

Fast Facts About the Program
- **Established:** 1910
- **Enrollment:** 39
- **Faculty:** 7 (all FT)
- **Student/Faculty Ratio:** 6:1
- **Degrees Conferred Since Inception:** 253
- **Degrees Conferred in 1991:** 7
- **Contact:** Dr. Robert J. McGraw, Chairman, Undergraduate Studies, 210 Waters Hall, University of Missouri–Columbia, Columbia, MO 65211; phone 314-882-6608

Fast Facts About the School
- State-supported coed university
- 1,335-acre campus in small-town setting
- **Enrollment:** 18,446
- **Faculty:** 1,804
- **Tuition:** State resident: $2442 to $3282; nonresident: $7302 to $8142
- **Fees:** $370
- **Room and Board:** $3160
- **Application Deadline:** 5/15
- **Entrance Difficulty Level:** Moderately difficult
- **Contact:** Georgeanne Porter, Director, Undergraduate Admissions, 314-882-7786

The Program
The mission of the program is to educate students in the study of plant and soil sciences as they apply to the growth of plants for human use. There is one named scholarship source for agronomy students. The University of Missouri–Columbia also offers programs in agricultural engineering and in agricultural mechanization and graduate programs in agronomy.

MAJOR/CONCENTRATIONS
Agronomy
Breeding and Physiology
Crop Production
Genetics
Land Use

Special Features
The College of Agriculture, Food, and Natural Resources operates several University farms. Three or 4 are used primarily by the department for field study. Upon graduation, all agronomy majors may be certified by the American Registry of Certified Professionals in agronomy, crops, and soils.

The Result
Graduates have a wide array of employment opportunities in agribusiness; production and management; state and federal agencies; extension, research, and teaching with educational institutions both within the United States and in international programs; and natural resource management in land use planning. Virtually all graduates find employment in their field or enroll in graduate school within 6 months of graduation.

Who's Recruiting Who on Campus
Employers: Cenex/Land O'Lakes, DeKalb Plant Genetics, Ciba-Geigy, Servi-Tech, Growmart, Bartlett & Co., American Cynamid, Golden Harvest/J.C. Robinson Co., USDA Soil Conservation Service, Northrup King Company. **Positions:** Seed and Crop Specialist, Feed Specialist, Crop Production Specialist, Sales Management Trainee, Production Management Trainee, Plant Supervisor, Grain Merchandiser, Soil Scientist.

UNIVERSITY OF NEW HAVEN
Environmental Science
West Haven, Connecticut

Fast Facts About the Program
- **Established:** 1972
- **Enrollment:** 42
- **Faculty:** 8 (7 FT, 1 PT)
- **Student/Faculty Ratio:** 5:1
- **Degrees Conferred Since Inception:** 70
- **Degrees Conferred in 1991:** 7
- **Contact:** Dr. R. Laurence Davis, Associate Professor, Department of Biology and Environmental Science, University of New Haven, 300 Orange Avenue, West Haven, CT 06516; phone 203-932-7108

Fast Facts About the School
- Independent comprehensive coed institution
- 73-acre campus in suburban setting
- **Enrollment:** 5,899
- **Faculty:** 424
- **Student/Faculty Ratio:** 15:1
- **Tuition:** $14,314
- **Fees:** $170
- **Room and Board:** $4744
- **Application Deadline:** 8/15
- **Entrance Difficulty Level:** Moderately difficult
- **Contact:** Steve Briggs, Dean of Admissions and Financial Aid, 203-932-7088 or 800-DIAL-UNH (out-of-state)

The Program

The B.S. in environmental science is a well-established program that has evolved over the years to provide a broad foundation for environmental scientists. The program incorporates the areas of biol-

MAJOR
Environmental Science

ogy, chemistry, physics, and math, as well as environmental science course work. It is felt that specialization within a particular field of environmental science is more appropriate at the graduate level and thus is an important component of the M.S. program in environmental science. The University's 5-year B.S./M.S. program provides an opportunity to complete both degrees in a reasonable period of time.

Special Features

A new geographical information system (GIS) laboratory supports the ARC/INFO software system that allows manipulation, display, and analysis of spacially referenced environmental data. Within a given geographical area, information regarding such things as soils, aquifers, land use, surface hydrology, critical habitats, population density, and zoning can be manipulated and correlated for activities such as environmental planning, management, and impact assessment. An environmental geological laboratory was recently established.

The Result

About 85% of graduates find employment in their field or continue on to advanced study within 6 months of graduation. The majority of graduates find employment with environmental testing, consulting, and/or remediation companies; municipal planning agencies; public environmental protection agencies; and the environmental planning and compliance departments of regional manufacturers.

Who's Recruiting Who on Campus
Employers: Olin, Pfizer Pharmaceuticals, Miles Laboratories, Lego

---

UNIVERSITY OF PITTSBURGH AT JOHNSTOWN
Biology/Ecology
Johnstown, Pennsylvania

Fast Facts About the Program
- **Established:** 1971
- **Enrollment:** 48
- **Faculty:** 4 (all FT)
- **Student/Faculty Ratio:** 12:1
- **Degrees Conferred Since Inception:** 200
- **Degrees Conferred in 1991:** 9
- **Contact:** Dennis M. McNair, Associate Professor/Coordinator, Department of Biology, University of Pittsburgh at Johnstown, Johnstown, PA 15904; phone 814-269-2907

Fast Facts About the School
- State-related 4-year coed college
- 650-acre campus in suburban setting
- **Enrollment:** 3,243
- **Faculty:** 201
- **Student/Faculty Ratio:** 20:1
- **Tuition:** State resident: $4290; nonresident: $9140
- **Fees:** $376
- **Room and Board:** $3394
- **Application Deadline:** Rolling
- **Entrance Difficulty Level:** Moderately difficult
- **Contact:** Thomas J. Wonders, Director, Admissions and Student Aid, 814-269-7076

The Program
Arranged around a biology core of introductory biology (2 semesters), genetics, and ecology, plus 4 semesters of chemistry, 2 semesters of physics, and 2 math courses (biostatistics and calculus), the curriculum is flexible and emphasizes interdisciplinary support (computer science, geography, geology, and others).

MAJOR/CONCENTRATION
Biology
Ecology

Special Features
The 600-acre nature preserve on campus is a mixed mesophytic forest suitable for a variety of research projects in aquatic and terrestrial ecology. The Pymatuning Laboratory of Ecology, the field station of the University of Pittsburgh, offers a wide variety of field courses and research opportunities during the summer months. The Biology Seminar Program brings in several speakers each term who have careers in some aspect of environmental biology. Internships have been established with various agencies and adjunct faculty members. Students are also encouraged to do research with faculty members in the department.

The Result
Most graduates go on to careers with federal and state governmental agencies, academic institutions, and private industry. A growing number pursue graduate work before launching their careers. In total, about 75% of all graduates find jobs or enter graduate school within 6 months of graduation.

Who's Recruiting Who on Campus
Employers (Positions): Pennsylvania Department of Resources (various positions); Pennsylvania Civil Service Commission (various positions); Quality Chemicals (Quality Controller); Geochemical Testing (Coal and Mineral Testers); Cambridge Biotechnology Corp. (Technician); International Technology Corp. (Technician); Kellman Associates (Environmental Impact Assessors)

UNIVERSITY OF VIRGINIA
Department of Environmental Sciences
Charlottesville, Virginia

Fast Facts About the Program
- **Established:** 1969
- **Enrollment:** 160
- **Faculty:** 40 (30 FT, 10 PT)
- **Student/Faculty Ratio:** 4:1
- **Degrees Conferred Since Inception:** 1,100
- **Degrees Conferred in 1991:** 76
- **Contact:** Judith Peatross, Director, Information Office, Department of Environmental Sciences, Clark Hall, University of Virginia, Charlottesville, VA 22903; phone 804-924-0527

Fast Facts About the School
- State-supported coed university
- 1,094-acre campus in suburban setting
- **Enrollment:** 17,606
- **Faculty:** 1,000
- **Student/Faculty Ratio:** 11:1
- **Tuition:** State resident: $3890; nonresident: $10,820
- **Room and Board:** $3620
- **Application Deadline:** 1/2
- **Entrance Difficulty Level:** Very difficult
- **Contact:** John A. Blackburn, Dean of Admissions, 804-924-7751

The Program

The major in environmental sciences gives students very strong preparation for employment, for entering professional schools, and for going to graduate school. All environmental sciences majors must complete 30 hours of graded course work in the department. Three of the 30 required credit hours may be taken from any of the 100- and 200-level noncore courses prior to the start of the third year. At least 11 hours must be advanced noncore courses at the 300-level or higher. Four core courses with labs are required of all majors. The department strongly encourages undergraduates to participate in research or fieldwork with faculty members and graduate students. Most research can be rewarded with course credit or wages.

MAJOR/CONCENTRATIONS

Environmental Sciences
Atmospheric Science
Ecology
Geology
Hydrology

Special Features

Department facilities include a new stable isotope laboratory with a mass spectrometer and a gas chromatograph interface, field vehicles, boats, aerial photographic interpretation equipment, an XRD laboratory, flumes, a wind tunnel, environmental chambers, analytical chemistry laboratories, greenhouse and insectory facilities, a NAFAX weather information line, and a GOES–Tap satellite receiver. Department field facilities include field enclosures for the study of small mammals, a completely instrumented watershed, and an instrumented lake. Recently, the department established the Virginia Coast Reserve/Long-Term Ecological Research site on Virginia's Eastern Shore. A laboratory/dormitory facility is located in Oyster, Virginia, and individuals from all disciplines in the department carry out research related to coastal systems through the program.

The Result

Approximately 66% of graduates find employment or enroll in graduate school within 6 months of graduation. Positions currently held by graduates include coastal research technician, groundwater construction manager, horticulturist, meteorologist, land-use attorney, coastal geologist, hydrogeologist, land-use planner, water quality manager, petroleum geophysicist, research biologist, hydrologist, plant pathologist, oceanographer, and air quality scientist.

UNIVERSITY OF WISCONSIN–GREEN BAY
Environmental Science
Green Bay, Wisconsin

Fast Facts About the Program
- **Established:** 1969
- **Enrollment:** 200
- **Faculty:** 17 (all PT)
- **Student/Faculty Ratio:** 12:1
- **Degrees Conferred Since Inception:** 300
- **Degrees Conferred in 1991:** 20
- **Contact:** Robert B. Wenger, Professor, Natural and Applied Sciences, University of Wisconsin–Green Bay, 2420 Nicolet Drive, Green Bay, WI 54311-7001; phone 414-465-2369

Fast Facts About the School
- State-supported comprehensive coed institution
- 700-acre campus in rural setting
- **Enrollment:** 5,423
- **Faculty:** 241
- **Student/Faculty Ratio:** 20:1
- **Tuition:** State resident: $1806; nonresident: $5660
- **Room and Board:** $2500
- **Application Deadline:** 4/15
- **Entrance Difficulty Level:** Moderately difficult
- **Contact:** Myron Van De Ven, Director, Admissions, 414-465-2111

The Program
The mission of the Environmental Science Program is to provide undergraduate students with an opportunity to study environmental problems and issues from an interdisciplinary perspective. The goal is to provide a cohesive, interdisciplinary program that enables students and faculty members to understand, analyze, and solve environmental problems. The program's focus is on scientific principles. The University of Wisconsin–Green Bay also offers a program in environmental policy and planning.

MAJOR/CONCENTRATIONS
Environmental Science
Ecology and Biological Resources Management
Physical Resources Management

Special Features
Facilities and resources located on campus that contribute significantly to the Environmental Science Program are the Richter Natural History Museum, an herbarium, a greenhouse, and the Cofrin Arboretum. A waste management/resource recovery laboratory provides research space for faculty members and students. A new instrumentation room houses several recently acquired and state-of-the-art instruments for conducting chemical analyses. Two natural areas, Toft's Point and Kingfisher Farm, are significant resources for field studies and student projects.

The Result
Some students go on to graduate study. The majority, however, move on to environmentally related positions in industry, consulting engineering firms, and public sector agencies.

Who's Recruiting Who on Campus
Employers (Positions): Champion International (Environmental Engineer); Menasha Corporation (Environmental Trainee); James River Corporation (Environmental Co-op); Environmental Marketing Services, Ltd. (Technical Sales/Service); Wisconsin Tissue Mills (Process Chemist); Wisconsin Department of Natural Resources (Environmental Intern, Environmental Specialist); Hazleton Laboratories (Research Assistant, Research Analyst)

WESTMINSTER COLLEGE
Environmental Science
New Wilmington, Pennsylvania

Fast Facts About the Program
- **Established:** 1978
- **Enrollment:** 32
- **Faculty:** 10 (9 FT, 1 PT)
- **Student/Faculty Ratio:** 3:1
- **Degrees Conferred Since Inception:** 37
- **Degrees Conferred in 1991:** 7
- **Contact:** Dr. Robert V. Travis, Coordinator of Environmental Science, Westminster College, New Wilmington, PA 16172; phone 412-946-7212

Fast Facts About the School
- Independent comprehensive coed institution, affiliated with Presbyterian Church (U.S.A.)
- 300-acre campus in small-town setting
- **Enrollment:** 1,554
- **Faculty:** 121
- **Student/Faculty Ratio:** 15:1
- **Tuition:** $11,210
- **Room and Board:** $3285
- **Application Deadline:** Rolling
- **Entrance Difficulty Level:** Moderately difficult
- **Contact:** Mr. R. Dana Paul, Director of Admissions, 412-946-7100

The Program
This interdisciplinary major is sponsored by the biology, chemistry, mathematics and computer science, and physics departments. Throughout their program, students are encouraged to become aware

> **MAJOR**
> Environmental Science

of the significance of other disciplines, such as economics, politics, the social sciences, and religion, on the study of the biosphere. A required senior capstone course is designed to further integrate science courses and liberal arts courses. The program consists of 18 designated and elective science courses. An internship, independent study, or honors research project is also required.

Special Features
Classes and labs are held in the Hoyt Science Resources Center, a state-of-the-art faculty-designed science building. Westminster students have hands-on laboratory experience using up-to-date equipment. Students participating in fieldwork have access to special on-campus outdoor facilities, such as a 40-acre beech and maple forest, a 40-acre outdoor laboratory, 2 creeks, and a 15-acre water impoundment. There are other special outdoor features within a 10-mile radius of campus, including an acid sphagnum bog and active and abandon strip mine areas.

The Result
Approximately 80% of majors find a job in their field or go on to pursue an advanced degree within 6 months of graduation. In the last 12 years, about a quarter of the graduates have sought advanced degrees at some of the best graduate schools in the country. They have entered programs in marine biology, entomology, water management, and environmental law. About a third of the graduates accepted jobs with U.S. government agencies, state environmental agencies, and private environmental consulting and/or testing companies as environmental scientists, solid-waste specialists, air quality specialists, and quality control specialists. Several have entered education fields. Westminster College gives students the opportunity to interact with professionals in the environmental science field. The College brings alumni and others to campus to speak directly to students about career potential in this field.

WILKES UNIVERSITY
Earth and Environmental Sciences
Wilkes-Barre, Pennsylvania

Fast Facts About the Program
- **Established:** 1978
- **Enrollment:** 65
- **Faculty:** 7 (6 FT, 1 PT)
- **Student/Faculty Ratio:** 9:1
- **Degrees Conferred Since Inception:** 75
- **Degrees Conferred in 1991:** 12
- **Environmental Library:** Yes
- **Contact:** Dale A. Bruns, Chair, GeoEnvironmental Science and Engineering, Wilkes University, Wilkes-Barre, PA 18766; phone 717-831-4614

Fast Facts About the School
- Independent comprehensive coed institution
- 25-acre campus in urban setting
- **Enrollment:** 3,432
- **Faculty:** 219
- **Student/Faculty Ratio:** 13:1
- **Tuition:** $9500
- **Fees:** $368
- **Room and Board:** $4500
- **Application Deadline:** Rolling
- **Entrance Difficulty Level:** Moderately difficult
- **Contact:** Emory Guffrovich, Dean of Admissions, 717-831-4400

The Program
The GeoEnvironmental Sciences and Engineering Department offers two major programs leading to Bachelor of Arts (B.A.) and Bachelor of Science (B.S.) degrees. Both programs incorporate a strong background in all of the sciences and include extensive laboratory and field experience. The interdisciplinary nature of the programs provides students with a unique breadth of understanding of the principles and concepts of the earth and environmental sciences while emphasizing methods of analysis and experimentation that are complex, dynamic, and interactive. Cooperative internships with environmental organizations and industries are encouraged.

MAJOR/CONCENTRATIONS

B.A. in Earth and Environmental Sciences
Business Administration
Earth and Space Science Teaching Certificate
Elementary Education
Political Science
Technical Writing

B.S. in Earth and Environmental Sciences
Air and Water Quality
Ecology
Field Biology
Geology

Special Features
Special features include 2 water-quality laboratories with atomic absorption spectroscopy, UV-vis spectroscopy, and portable field analysis instrumentation; an air quality laboratory with meteorological equipment and a Miran (IR) portable organic vapor analyzer; a gas chromatography/mass spectroscopy laboratory; a rock and mineral laboratory with mineral collection; a plant herbarium; insect/invertebrate collections; a 120-acre field research station with a solar-designed environmental home, lake, fields, stream, and forest habitats; an astronomy observatory; natural floodplain forest on Susquehanna River; and wetlands natural areas. Students are encouraged to particpate in cooperative education or internships with agencies and industry and must complete a senior research project.

The Result
The major leading to the B.S. degree emphasizes the technical and analytical aspects of the earth and environmental sciences. The major leading to the B.A. degree emphasizes human interactions with earth and environmental sciences. Eighty to 90% of graduates enroll in graduate school or find a job in their field within 6 months of graduation.

WILLIAM PATERSON COLLEGE OF NEW JERSEY
Environmental Science
Wayne, New Jersey

Fast Facts About the Program
- **Established:** 1976
- **Enrollment:** 40
- **Faculty:** 4 (3 FT, 1 PT)
- **Student/Faculty Ratio:** 10:1
- **Degrees Conferred Since Inception:** 21
- **Degrees Conferred in 1991:** 2
- **Contact:** Dr. Richard Pardi, Department of Environmental Science and Geography, William Paterson College of New Jersey, Wayne, NJ 07470; phone 201-595-3464

Fast Facts About the School
- State-supported comprehensive coed institution
- 250-acre campus in small-town setting
- **Enrollment:** 9,706
- **Faculty:** 318
- **Student/Faculty Ratio:** 14:1
- **Tuition:** State resident: $1908; nonresident: $2508
- **Room and Board:** $4250
- **Application Deadline:** 6/30
- **Entrance Difficulty Level:** Moderately difficult
- **Contact:** Leo DeBartolo, Director of Admissions, 201-595-2906

The Program
The program includes basic courses in the natural sciences and more advanced courses relating the natural sciences to environmental concerns. For the Senior Practicum, students use their training in

MAJOR
Environmental Science

a real case study of some specific environmental problem for a local community. The program also includes a formal cooperative education (field experience) component.

Special Features
Major equipment includes a mass spectrometer/gas chromatograph; transmission and scanning electron microscopes (with X-ray analyzer); UV-visible and infrared spectrometers; a 200-MHz NMR spectrometer; 5 gas and high-pressure liquid chromatographs; an inductively coupled plasma emission spectrograph; an ion chromatograph; low-, high-, and ultrahigh-speed centrifuges; a liquid scintillation counter; electrophoresis instrumentation; a refrigerated fraction collector; a seismometer; a research greenhouse; and an ecology lab with both stationary and field equipment. State-of-the-art minicomputer and microcomputer networks are part of the Science Complex. Students also have access to software programs specifically geared to environmental science issues.

The Result
Students are prepared for entry-level positions in research, manufacturing, sales, and management. Potential employers include government agencies, private consulting firms, and industries dealing with environmental problems. Students may also pursue K–12 teacher certification. A large part of the recruitment process is the contacts students make at the departmentally sponsored Environmental Career Days. Career Day participants vary but are usually from the surrounding New Jersey area. Virtually all majors find employment in their field or go on to advanced study within 6 months of graduation.

Environmental
Studies

Environmental studies is a broad program that involves the study of physical sciences, social sciences, and humanities to analyze a wide variety of environmental issues as they relate to policymaking, planning, and management of the earth's resources.

BEMIDJI STATE UNIVERSITY
Environmental Studies
Bemidji, Minnesota

Fast Facts About the Program
- **Established:** 1968
- **Enrollment:** 84
- **Faculty:** 12 (all FT)
- **Student/Faculty Ratio:** 7:1
- **Degrees Conferred Since Inception:** 200
- **Degrees Conferred in 1991:** 8
- **Contact:** Dr. Steven Spigarelli, Director of Center for Environmental Studies, Sattgast Hall, Bemidji State University, Bemidji, MN 56601; phone 218-755-2910

Fast Facts About the School
- State-supported comprehensive coed institution
- 83-acre campus in small-town setting
- **Enrollment:** 5,401
- **Faculty:** 220
- **Student/Faculty Ratio:** 19:1
- **Tuition:** State resident: $1882; nonresident: $3521
- **Fees:** $269
- **Room and Board:** $2490
- **Application Deadline:** 8/15
- **Entrance Difficulty Level:** Moderately difficult
- **Contact:** Paul Muller, Associate Director of Admissions, 218-755-2040

The Program
The major is designed to provide students with an awareness and understanding of environmental relationships and the interactions between human activity and the natural world in which that activity occurs. The program prepares students for employment by industry and government in positions concerned with pollution abatement and environmental protection. Environmental studies majors are required to complete core courses and a field of emphasis. This allows students to develop an extensive background in disciplines that relate to environmental understanding and protection as well as an intensive background in the student's area of interest.

MAJOR/CONCENTRATIONS
Environment
  Ecosystems Studies (Biology Minor)
  Environmental Chemistry (Chemistry Minor)
  Environmental Policy and Planning
  Geohydrology

Special Features
Special features include the Hebson Memorial Forest, which has tree plantations and peat bogs, and an aquatic laboratory.

The Result
Seventy percent of graduates find employment or enroll in graduate school within 6 months of graduation. Students find careers in federal, state, and local environmental regulatory agencies; in industrial pollution abatement and pollution prevention programs; and after subsequent graduate training, in research in environmental health and toxicology.

Who's Recruiting Who on Campus
Employers: U.S. Forest Service; U.S. and Minnesota Department of Natural Resources; Environmental Protection Agency; Minnesota Pollution Control; Minnesota mining industries, especially iron mining

BOWLING GREEN STATE UNIVERSITY
Environmental Policy and Analysis
Bowling Green, Ohio

Fast Facts About the Program
- **Established:** 1980
- **Enrollment:** 83
- **Faculty:** 35 (30 FT, 5 PT)
- **Student/Faculty Ratio:** 2:1
- **Degrees Conferred Since Inception:** 100
- **Degrees Conferred in 1991:** 16
- **Environmental Library Holdings:** 10,000 bound volumes; 86 periodical subscriptions; 65 records/tapes/CDs
- **Contact:** Thomas B. Cobb, Director, Center for Environmental Programs, 153 College Park Office Building, Bowling Green, OH 43403; phone 419-372-8207

Fast Facts About the School
- State-supported coed university
- 1,176-acre campus in small-town setting
- **Enrollment:** 17,960
- **Faculty:** 913
- **Student/Faculty Ratio:** 20:1
- **Tuition:** State resident: $2506; nonresident: $6724
- **Fees:** $554
- **Room and Board:** $2686
- **Application Deadline:** Rolling
- **Entrance Difficulty Level:** Moderately difficult
- **Contact:** John W. Martin, Director of Admissions, 419-372-2086

The Program
The Environmental Policy and Analysis Program was developed for students with a commitment to environmental quality and an interest in administrative, legislative, and organizational problems. It provides the basic scientific skills and social and behavioral knowledge needed to work in areas dealing with the development, interpretation, and administration of environmental policy and law.

MAJOR/CONCENTRATIONS
Environmental Policy and Analysis
Economics of Energy and Environment
Economics of Regulated Industries
Environmental Administration
Environmental Management
Environmental Planning
Natural Areas and Preserves Management
Outdoor Education

Special Features
Students in this program can select an internship with the Washington Center in a legislator's office or with an environmental organization or company. Students often find summer positions through the center's Summer Intern Recommendation Program with national park and historic areas, camps, and outdoor education centers. A distinguished speakers series brings programs to campus that feature leaders of environmental organizations, legislators, and activists. Students are encouraged to attend dinners with these guests for a one-on-one experience.

The Result
Graduates typically find positions working with issues such as changing patterns of land use and development, protection of wilderness, restoration of land following resource extraction, and preservation of unique areas and endangered species and as nontraditional educators.

Who's Recruiting Who on Campus
Employers: Peace Corps; Sherwin-Williams Paints; Glidden Co.; ENSR Operations; Brukner Nature Center; Hurley, Schnauffer & Associates; Toledo Edison Company

EAST STROUDSBURG UNIVERSITY OF PENNSYLVANIA
Environmental Studies
East Stroudsburg, Pennsylvania

Fast Facts About the Program
- **Established:** 1972
- **Enrollment:** 100
- **Faculty:** 10 (all FT)
- **Student/Faculty Ratio:** 10:1
- **Degrees Conferred Since Inception:** 750
- **Degrees Conferred in 1991:** 25
- **Contact:** Dr. L. M. Rymon, Coordinator of Environmental Studies, East Stroudsburg University of Pennsylvania, East Stroudsburg, PA 18301; phone 717-424-3714

Fast Facts About the School
- State-supported comprehensive coed institution
- 183-acre campus in small-town setting
- **Enrollment:** 5,494
- **Faculty:** 277
- **Student/Faculty Ratio:** 20:1
- **Tuition:** State resident: $3388; nonresident: $5952
- **Fees:** $460
- **Room and Board:** $3120
- **Application Deadline:** 3/1
- **Entrance Difficulty Level:** Moderately difficult
- **Contact:** Alan T. Chesterton, Director of Admissions, 717-424-3542

The Program
This program offers an integrated interdisciplinary course of study within the tradition of liberal education at East Stroudsburg. The curriculum is intended to provide students with the knowledge of

MAJOR
Environmental Studies

different disciplines as they study the environment. The program at East Stroudsburg has been designed to meet the needs of state, local, and federal organizations as well as those of private industry, and flexibility has become the guide that allows access within and between academic divisions and departments.

Special Features
Students in the life sciences are afforded opportunities to conduct studies on 2 ecology preserves held by the University. In addition, the campus is close to the 72,000-acre Delaware Water Gap National Recreation Area. The internship is one of the most important components of the student's curriculum. Students have served as interns with private, local, state, and federal agencies. They have assumed duties from coast to coast, in Canada, and overseas. Each student is expected to learn, under the supervision of the host agency, the daily routine and long-term functions of that agency. Evaluations are based on reports and the student's log. The acquisition of an internship is a cooperative venture among the student, the adviser, and the sponsor.

The Result
Graduates of this program are prepared to serve as naturalists in the National Park Service, as rangers in the Forestry Service, as lab technicians, as environmental control officers in the Environmental Protection Agency, and as Peace Corps volunteers. About 50% to 60% of graduates find employment in their field or enroll in graduate school within 6 months of graduation.

FLORIDA INTERNATIONAL UNIVERSITY
Environmental Studies
Miami, Florida

Fast Facts About the Program
- **Established:** 1972
- **Enrollment:** 180
- **Faculty:** 22 (20 FT, 2 PT)
- **Student/Faculty Ratio:** 8:1
- **Degrees Conferred Since Inception:** 190
- **Degrees Conferred in 1991:** 25
- **Contact:** Dr. John Parker, Director, Chemistry Department, Florida International University, Miami, FL 33199; phone 305-348-1930

Fast Facts About the School
- State-supported coed university
- 544-acre campus in urban setting
- **Enrollment:** 23,841
- **Faculty:** 1,082
- **Student/Faculty Ratio:** 18:1
- **Tuition:** State resident: $1404; nonresident: $5543
- **Fees:** $74
- **Room and Board:** $3490
- **Application deadline:** 6/1
- **Entrance Difficulty Level:** Moderately difficult
- **Contact:** Ms. Carmen Brown, Director of Admissions, 305-348-2363

The Program
Academic training for both Bachelor of Arts and Bachelor of Science degrees is interdisciplinary since the program deals more with global systems than with traditional academic boundaries.

Special Features
The Environmental Colloquium, taken 3 times by all majors, provides guest speakers from local, state, federal, and international agencies and businesses, giving students job and academic contact opportunities. The FIU Preserve is a 7-acre tract that is used for instruction in ecology, environmental education, and environmental restoration.

The Result
About 75% of graduates find employment or enroll in graduate school within six months of graduation. Many enter Dade County or Florida State environmental agencies in positions as wastewater technicians, solid-waste monitors, and urban wildlife specialists or join local firms as environmental monitors or analysts. Others enter graduate programs in biology, landscape architecture, law, and urban planning.

MAJORS/CONCENTRATIONS
B.A. in Environmental Studies
Energy
Human Ecology
International Political Issues
Resource Management
Urban Policy/Planning

B.S. in Environmental Studies
Air, Water, or Energy Resources
Computer Sciences
Geology
Marine Sciences
Organismal Biology
Quantitative Ecology

Who's Recruiting Who on Campus

Employers (Positions): U.S. Bureau of Land Management (Botanists, Soil Science Technicians, Solid Waste Monitors); U.S. Forestry Service (Rangers, Botanists, Wildlife Biologists); Environmental Protection Agency (Graduate Research Interns, Project Technicians); National Park Service (Rangers, Wildlife Biologists, Wetlands Managers)

FROSTBURG STATE UNIVERSITY
Environmental Analysis and Planning
Frostburg, Maryland

Fast Facts About the Program
- **Established:** 1980
- **Enrollment:** 84
- **Faculty:** 12 (all FT)
- **Student/Faculty Ratio:** 7:1
- **Degrees Conferred Since Inception:** 35
- **Degrees Conferred in 1991:** 5
- **Contact:** William Nizinski, Chairman, Department of Geography, Frostburg State University, Frostburg, MD 21532; phone 301-689-4369

Fast Facts About the School
- State-supported comprehensive coed institution
- 260-acre campus in small-town setting
- **Enrollment:** 5,239
- **Faculty:** 300
- **Student/Faculty Ratio:** 17:1
- **Tuition:** State resident: $2222; nonresident: $4210
- **Fees:** $540
- **Room and Board:** $4290
- **Application Deadline:** Rolling
- **Entrance Difficulty Level:** Moderately difficult
- **Contact:** David Sanford, Dean of Admissions, 301-689-4201

The Program

The goal of the Environmental Analysis and Planning (EAP) Program is to provide students with the knowledge and tools necessary to bridge the gap between natural resource development and envi-

> **MAJOR**
> **Environmental Analysis and Planning**

ronmental protection. Students develop many skills, such as stormwater management, wetland delineation, site analysis, surveying, cartography, drafting, and computer operations. Students obtain internships in a variety of professional offices, including the Maryland Bureau of Mines and the Soil Conservation Service.

Special Features

The resources available include a well-equipped cartography lab complete with computer facilities and applicable software and equipment and facilities needed for surveying and field investigations. An EPA-certified water quality lab and a soils analysis lab also provide valuable support to the program. Extensive map, aerial photograph, and satellite imagery collections are housed in both the department and the FSU library. The library serves as a map depository for the U.S. Geological Survey and Defense Mapping Agency. One of the most significant features of the program, however, is the local environment. This environment, which is composed of forest, wetlands, streams, lakes, land disturbed by development, and disturbed land that has been reclaimed, provides students with an excellent opportunity to study firsthand the need, importance, and opportunities of environmental planning and reclamation.

The Result

EAP majors obtain employment with regulatory agencies, soil conservation services, highway departments, land developers, surveyors, mining companies, engineering companies, environmental consulting firms, and planning commissions. About 90% of graduates find a job in their field or go on to advanced studies within 6 months of graduation.

INDIANA UNIVERSITY BLOOMINGTON
Public Affairs
Bloomington, Indiana

Fast Facts About the Program
- **Established:** 1972
- **Enrollment:** 115
- **Faculty:** 15 (7 FT, 8 PT)
- **Student/Faculty Ratio:** 8:1
- **Degrees Conferred Since Inception:** 125
- **Degrees Conferred in 1991:** 27
- **Contact:** Roger B. Parks, Director, Undergraduate Programs, School of Public and Environmental Affairs, Indiana University Bloomington, Bloomington, IN 47405; phone 812-855-3475

Fast Facts About the School
- State-supported coed university
- 1,800-acre campus in small-town setting
- **Enrollment:** 35,489
- **Faculty:** 1,653
- **Tuition:** State resident: $2390; nonresident: $7678
- **Fees:** $200 to $255
- **Room and Board:** $3370
- **Application Deadline:** 2/15
- **Entrance Difficulty Level:** Moderately difficult
- **Contact:** Robert Magee, Director of Admissions, 812-855-0661

The Program

The environmental programs at the School of Public and Environmental Affairs (SPEA) are designed to train professionals who will be able to successfully fuse scientific, policy, and management perspectives while helping to develop and implement sound solutions to the environmental problems of the global community. Since the school's founding in 1972, it has emphasized the integration of policy, regulation, and social good with an understanding of environmental science necessary for future public servants. Environmental science and management students are required to develop a background in laboratory science (biology, chemistry, geology) as well as in economics, law, management, and policy analysis while also completing the normal requirements of a liberal education.

MAJOR/CONCENTRATIONS
Public Affairs
Environmental Science and Management
Management
Public Financial Management
Public Policy
Specialized concentrations are developed individually with a faculty adviser

Special Features

SPEA has extensive laboratory facilities for environmental science studies, including laboratories for groundwater modeling, wetlands, ecology, and trace metals. Off-campus facilities include the Hoosier National Forest, Brown and Morgan-Monroe state forests, and Monroe and Griffy lakes, all within a few miles of campus. The colloquium series brings professionals in the environment and other fields together for formal and informal discussions with students and faculty. Students pursue a variety of internships.

The Result

About 67% of graduates enroll in graduate school or find employment within 6 months of graduation. SPEA graduates with an environmental science and management concentration divide roughly into those who pursue graduate degrees immediately; those who accept specialized positions in public organizations dealing with water resources, wetlands, air pollution, and similar technical fields; and those who accept positions with private consulting firms and nonprofit organizations. Recent public placements include the Indiana Department of Environmental Management and the U.S. Environmental Protection Agency. Consulting firms and not-for-profits include Entrix, ATEC, and the Wilderness Society.

NORTHEASTERN ILLINOIS UNIVERSITY
Environmental Studies
Chicago, Illinois

Fast Facts About the Program
- **Established:** 1977
- **Enrollment:** 62
- **Faculty:** 9 (8 FT, 1 PT)
- **Student/Faculty Ratio:** 7:1
- **Degrees Conferred Since Inception:** 124
- **Degrees Conferred in 1991:** 6
- **Contact:** Barbara J. Winston, Department Chair, Northeastern Illinois University, 5500 N. St. Louis, Chicago, IL 60625; phone 312-794-2609

Fast Facts About the School
- State-supported comprehensive coed institution
- 67-acre campus in urban setting
- **Enrollment:** 11,274
- **Faculty:** 542
- **Student/Faculty Ratio:** 18:1
- **Tuition:** State resident: $1656; nonresident: $4968
- **Fees:** $423
- **Application Deadline:** 8/1
- **Entrance Difficulty Level:** Minimally difficult
- **Contact:** Miriam Rivera, Acting Director of Admissions and Records, 312-583-4050 Ext. 3663

The Program

Northeastern Illinois's program is multidisciplinary as well as issue oriented and prepares students for employment as environmental professionals in a variety of subsidiary fields. To earn the degree, students must complete at least 15 credit hours of core

MAJOR/CONCENTRATIONS

Environmental Studies
Environmental Interpretation/Education
Environmental Planning/Management

requirements and 30 credit hours of approved courses. An environmental planning/management concentration prepares students for positions in energy or water resources, solid waste, natural areas, resource development, and environmental lobbying. Students who pursue an environmental interpretation/education specialty qualify for employment as naturalists or as environmental educators, among other positions.

Special Features

Students benefit from state-of-the-art equipment in developing skills in computer mapping, aerial photography, and satellite image interpretation. Students have access to numerous environmental organizations, government agencies, and businesses in the Chicago metropolitan area for independent study, internships, and jobs.

The Result

Program graduates obtain entry-level positions in fields such as natural area management/planning, solid-waste program development/coordination, urban forestry, floodplain and wastewater management, environmental auditing, permitting and impact assessment, environmental interpretation and education, urban and regional planning, computer mapping, and environmental advocacy. While working in the environmental field, many students pursue the Master of Arts in Geography and Environmental Studies degree.

Who's Recruiting Who on Campus

Employers: Illinois and U.S. Environmental Protection agencies, Federal Emergency Management Agency, U.S. Department of Agriculture Forest Service, the McHenry County Defenders, the Nature Conservancy, the Illinois Environmental Council

---

PRESCOTT COLLEGE
Environmental Studies
Prescott, Arizona

Fast Facts About the Program
- **Established:** 1966
- **Enrollment:** 147
- **Faculty:** 12 (8 FT, 4 PT)
- **Student/Faculty Ratio:** 12:1
- **Degrees Conferred Since Inception:** 110
- **Degrees Conferred in 1991:** 8
- **Contact:** Dr. Mark Riegner, Program Coordinator, Prescott College, 220-EE Grove Ave., Prescott, AZ 86301; phone 602-776-5183

Fast Facts About the School
- Independent comprehensive coed institution
- 4-acre campus in small-town setting
- **Enrollment:** 330
- **Faculty:** 54
- **Student/Faculty Ratio:** 10:1
- **Tuition:** $7800
- **Fees:** $145
- **Room and Board:** Not available
- **Application Deadline:** Rolling
- **Entrance Difficulty Level:** Moderately difficult
- **Contact:** Shari Sterling, Assistant Director of Admissions, 602-778-2090 Ext. 127

The Program
The Environmental Studies Program embraces a host of disciplines that stem from environmental, biological, and human sciences. Studies focus on the interrelationships between the human and non-human worlds and their reciprocal influences. Students in the program develop an understanding of the complex interrelationships in the natural world, recognize the role of humans in these interrelationships, develop specific skills in field research methods and critical thinking, and become capable of taking appropriate action based on carefully considered values.

MAJORS
Environmental Conservation
Environmental Design
Environmental Education and Interpretation
Environment and Economics
Geography
Human Ecology
Natural History
Wilderness Studies

Special Features
The great biological diversity of the Southwest is the focus of many field courses. Prescott National Forest provides local opportunities for field studies and for internships in wilderness management with the National Forest Service. Due to its proximity to Mexico, the program is able to offer courses on coastal and cultural ecology of the Gulf of California and is currently developing a field station in Kino Bay, Mexico. The program's international focus extends to Costa Rica, where courses are offered regularly. Students are encouraged to undertake self-directed studies and internships, and they have participated in learning experiences in North and Central America in a variety of fields.

The Result
Graduate jobs include Director of Education at a Museum of Natural History, environmental journalist, field biologist, interpretive naturalist for the Park Service, environmental consultant for Endangered Species Management, high school science teacher, and Director of Nature Center. One graduate won the John Burroughs award for Naturalist Writing and a MacArthur Foundation award for his work on ethnobotany.

SAN JOSE STATE UNIVERSITY
Environmental Studies
San Jose, California

Fast Facts About the Program
- **Established:** 1970
- **Enrollment:** 330
- **Faculty:** 8 (6 FT, 2 PT)
- **Student/Faculty Ratio:** 41:1
- **Degrees Conferred Since Inception:** 2,000
- **Degrees Conferred in 1991:** 50
- **Environmental Library Holdings:** 2,000 bound volumes; 50 periodical subscriptions
- **Contact:** Lester Roundtree, Director, Environmental Studies Program, WSQ 118, San Jose State University, San Jose, CA 95192-0116; phone 408-924-5450

Fast Facts About the School
- State-supported comprehensive coed institution
- 104-acre campus in urban setting
- **Enrollment:** 30,061
- **Faculty:** 1,636
- **Student/Faculty Ratio:** 16:1
- **Tuition:** State resident: $0; nonresident: $7380
- **Fees:** $1184
- **Room and Board:** $4244
- **Application Deadline:** Rolling
- **Entrance Difficulty Level:** Moderately difficult
- **Contact:** Edgar Chambers, Associate Executive Vice-President, Admissions and Records, 408-924-2009

The Program

San Jose State's Environmental Studies Program offers both a B.A. and B.S. degree. The former is designed for people emphasizing the social science aspect of environmental studies, while the latter is for those who wish a hard science background. The B.S. degree program is 132 semester units, which is 8 more than the B.A. program. Each degree program has 3 components: preparation for the major, which includes courses in chemistry, biology, and economics; the environmental studies core program, which consists of classes (environmental economics, law, human ecology, and resources), a seminar, and a thesis; and the emphasis or concentration, which is roughly 32 semester units focused on a specific topic.

MAJOR/CONCENTRATIONS

B.A. or B.S. in Environmental Studies
Ecological Systems
Energy Management
Environmental Planning
Groundwater Resources
Hazardous Waste
Integrated Waste Management
Water Resources
Wildlife Management
Self-designed concentration

Special Features

Probably the most important and effective special feature of this program is the emphasis placed on internships with local governmental agencies, industry, and environmental groups. Each student must take at least 6 semester units of internships, which give each student a real-world experience and on-the-job training. This component may account for the fact that graduates have a very high success rate in finding employment soon after graduation.

The Result

The Environmental Studies Program has the second-best employment record at San Jose State University. Approximately 90% of graduates find employment in their field or go on to advanced studies within 6 months of graduation. Some typical jobs held by recent graduates are water resource planner, environmental planner, solar energy consultant, energy auditor, energy conservation specialist, environmental review coordinator, and integrated waste manager.

SONOMA STATE UNIVERSITY
Environmental Studies and Planning
Rohnert Park, California

Fast Facts About the Program
- **Established:** 1972
- **Enrollment:** 300
- **Faculty:** 12 (5 FT, 7 PT)
- **Student/Faculty Ratio:** 25:1
- **Degrees Conferred Since Inception:** 750
- **Degrees Conferred in 1991:** 60
- **Contact:** Dr. W. J. Rohwedder, Chair, Department of Environmental Studies and Planning, Sonoma State University, Rohnert Park, CA 94928; phone 707-664-2306

Fast Facts About the School
- State-supported comprehensive coed institution
- 220-acre campus in small-town setting
- **Enrollment:** 7,557
- **Faculty:** 449
- **Student/Faculty Ratio:** 17:1
- **Tuition:** State resident: $0; nonresident: $7380
- **Fees:** $936
- **Room and Board:** $4800
- **Application Deadline:** 11/1
- **Entrance Difficulty Level:** Moderately difficult
- **Contact:** Dr. Frank Tansey, Dean of Admissions, 707-664-2778

The Program
The program of study integrates knowledge from a variety of disciplines in helping students to understand the function of ecological systems and the nature of human impact upon these systems. All students receive fundamental instruction related to ecology and the environment based on knowledge from the biological, physical, and social sciences and the humanities. This broad understanding is applied to a particular area of environmental concern through the student's concentration. Career-oriented study plans are offered in environmental conservation and restoration, environmental education, environmental technology, and in the planning concentration (city and regional planning). As part of their course of study, all students complete a senior project or internship.

MAJOR/CONCENTRATIONS
Environmental Studies and Planning
Environmental Conservation and Restoration
Environmental Education
Environmental Technology
Planning

Special Features
EarthLab is an education and demonstration center that focuses on sustainable agriculture and energy. The EarthLab includes an energy-efficient building complex, herb gardens, composting demonstrations, a handicap-access garden, a children's garden, an outdoor classroom, a solar cooker demonstration, and much more. Workshops and tours are offered to members of the campus and the surrounding community. The Resource Room is a lending center containing ENSP equipment for environmental investigation and research.

The Result
Seventy-five percent of graduates find employment or enroll in graduate school within 6 months of graduation. Graduates have found employment in public and private educational facilities, city and regional planning agencies, law and natural resource management, and energy management. Students enter graduate programs in environmental sciences, law, architecture, engineering, public policy, and planning.

SOUTHERN VERMONT COLLEGE
Environmental Studies
Bennington, Vermont

Fast Facts About the Program
- **Established:** 1976
- **Enrollment:** 55
- **Faculty:** 6
- **Student/Faculty Ratio:** 9:1
- **Degrees Conferred Since Inception:** 160
- **Degrees Conferred in 1991:** 8
- **Contact:** Dr. Verne B. Howe, Director, Environmental Studies, Southern Vermont College, Bennington, VT 05201; phone 802-442-5427

Fast Facts About the School
- Independent 4-year coed college
- 371-acre campus in small-town setting
- **Enrollment:** 726
- **Faculty:** 69
- **Student/Faculty Ratio:** 18:1
- **Tuition:** $7740
- **Fees:** $282
- **Room and Board:** $4180
- **Application Deadline:** Rolling
- **Entrance Difficulty Level:** Minimally difficult
- **Contact:** Mary Van Arsdale, Director of Admissions, 802-442-5427 Ext. 138

The Program
The study of ecology is the scientific base used for environmental studies. Required courses include ecology with lab, economics, environmental ethics, environmental history, environmental law, environmental policy and politics, and land use planning as well as a minimum of 4 other natural science courses with a lab. Students are encouraged to take cartography and statistics as electives. (Students taking a minor are not required to take all of the above.) The capstone course is the senior seminar, during which students work with faculty members and experts outside the College on a research project.

MAJORS/CONCENTRATIONS
Environmental Management
Environmental Studies
Criminal Justice and the Environment
English
Environmental Communications

Special Features
The College is located on a side of Mt. Anthony where there are over 300 acres of forest land that are used by the program. Streams, ponds, and lakes in Bennington are used by students as well. Internships are available with local, state, and federal agencies as well as with area businesses. A new cooperative program gives students the opportunity to spend 2 semesters with the Green Mountain National Forest Service. The College also offers a semester-abroad program. On campus, speakers are featured not only in class but during special events. Earth Day, planned and managed by environmental studies students since 1990, is one such event. In addition, an effort is made to provide students with opportunities to attend environmental conferences in the region.

The Result
Graduates have been placed in wastewater management, water treatment, risk assessment, cartography, and land use planning positions at local and regional levels. Graduates work with state agencies of natural resources and within the federal system. Some teach. Many students go on to graduate school. Within 6 months of graduation, 85% of students in these majors find employment in their field or go on to pursue an advanced degree.

SOUTHWEST TEXAS STATE UNIVERSITY
Resource and Environmental Studies
San Marcos, Texas

Fast Facts About the Program	Fast Facts About the School
• **Established:** 1965 • **Enrollment:** 240 • **Faculty:** 14 (all FT) • **Student/Faculty Ratio:** 17:1 • **Degrees Conferred Since Inception:** 1,175 • **Degrees Conferred in 1991:** 72 • **Contact:** Dr. Richard G. Boehm, Chairman, Department of Geography and Planning, Southwest Texas State University, San Marcos, TX 78666-4614; phone 512-245-2170	• State-supported comprehensive coed institution • 383-acre campus in small-town setting • **Enrollment:** 21,743 • **Faculty:** 881 • **Student/Faculty Ratio:** 22:1 • **Tuition:** State resident: $720; nonresident: $3840 • **Fees:** $686 • **Room and Board:** $3298 • **Application Deadline:** 7/1 • **Entrance Difficulty Level:** Moderately difficult • **Contact:** Marilissa Morgan, Director, Admissions, 512-245-2364 Ext. 2803

The Program

The program in applied geography prepares students for positions in resource conservation and environmental management. The program applies geographic content and methods to problems of air, land, and water pollution; transportation; energy; water resources; and land development.

MAJOR/CONCENTRATIONS

Resource and Environmental Studies
Cartography/Geographic Information Systems
Urban and Regional Planning

The program requires 30 hours for the Bachelor of Arts degree. An internship is required.

Special Features

The department is housed on two floors of a modern facility adjacent to the University's new 7-floor library and near the new science center. Four computer laboratories with state-of-the-art computer equipment for both cartography and geographic information systems are dedicated to the department. The campus is located in the center of the 100-mile-long Austin/San Antonio corridor, which serves as a laboratory for problems of growth management related to surface water and groundwater quality, endangered species, and a variety of other problems of national and global significance. The University owns adjacent ranch land, which is useful for research purposes.

The Result

Graduates are currently employed as resource managers, environmental impact specialists, demographers, cartographers, community development specialists, regional planners, land-use planners, and earth scientists. Eighty percent of graduates find employment in their field or enroll in graduate school within 6 months of graduation.

Who's Recruiting Who on Campus

Employers (Positions): municipal and county governments (Environmental Specialist, Geographic Information Systems Specialist); Texas Department of Water Resources (Permit Specialist, Environmental Manager, Water Quality Specialist, Solid-Waste Specialist)

SUNY COLLEGE OF ENVIRONMENTAL SCIENCE AND FORESTRY

Environmental Studies

Syracuse, New York

Fast Facts About the Program	**Fast Facts About the School**
• **Established:** 1971	• State-supported coed university
• **Enrollment:** 219	• 12-acre campus in urban setting
• **Faculty:** 9 (8 FT, 1 PT)	• **Enrollment:** 1,551
• **Student/Faculty Ratio:** 24:1	• **Faculty:** 122
• **Degrees Conferred Since Inception:** 1,312	• **Student/Faculty Ratio:** 20:1
• **Degrees Conferred in 1991:** 76	• **Tuition:** State resident: $2650; nonresident: $6250
• **Contact:** Dr. Ralph A. Sanders, Chair, Environmental Studies, SUNY College of Environmental Science and Forestry, Syracuse, NY 13210; phone 315-470-6636	• **Fees:** $287
	• **Room and Board:** $5845
	• **Application Deadline:** Rolling
	• **Entrance Difficulty Level:** Very difficult
	• **Contact:** Susan Sanford, Associate Director of Admissions, 315-470-6600

The Program

The mission of the Environmental Studies Program is to provide students with a holistic, integrated education in environmental matters and concerns. This is done by studying natural systems; quantification and analysis; the impact of humans on resources and systems and the social processes involved; the manner in which society manages these systems and the institutional arrangements; and the ethical value systems that help to form and guide human activity and the response to environmental issues.

MAJOR/CONCENTRATIONS

Environmental Studies
Biological Science Applications
Information and Technology
Land Use Planning
Policy and Management

Special Features

The SUNY College of Environmental Science and Forestry (ESF) enjoys an international reputation and maintains 25,000 acres at campuses and field stations throughout the state. The college provides students and faculty with all the advantages of the SUNY system and adjacent Syracuse University, as well as one of the most intimate atmospheres of any doctoral granting institution. Students at ESF also mix with Syracuse University students in classrooms on both campuses, and at the school's top-notch facilities.

The Result

Graduates from this program pursue graduate studies in public administration, law, planning, biology, water resources, solid-waste management, environmental engineering, water quality management, and public policy. Some pertinent job titles of 1991 graduates are environmental coordinator, environmental biologist, environmental scientist, education adviser–sanitation, research specialist, and research laboratory assistant.

Who's Recruiting Who on Campus

Employers: Niagra Mohawk Power Corporation, U.S. Soil Conservation Service, U.S. Army Corps of Engineers, U.S. Environmental Protection Agency

---

STOCKTON STATE COLLEGE
Environmental Studies
Pomona, New Jersey

Fast Facts About the Program
- **Established:** 1973
- **Enrollment:** 232
- **Faculty:** 9 (8 FT, 1 PT)
- **Student/Faculty Ratio:** 26:1
- **Degrees Conferred Since Inception:** 1,011
- **Degrees Conferred in 1991:** 36
- **Contact:** Dr. Michael Geller, Environmental Studies Program Coordinator, Stockton State College, Pomona, NJ 08240; phone 609-652-4620

Fast Facts About the School
- State-supported 4-year coed college
- 1,600-acre campus in small-town setting
- **Enrollment:** 4,965
- **Faculty:** 288
- **Student/Faculty Ratio:** 17:1
- **Tuition:** State resident: $1984; nonresident: $3096
- **Fees:** $472
- **Room and Board:** $3840
- **Application Deadline:** 5/1
- **Entrance Difficulty Level:** Very difficult
- **Contact:** Salvatore Catalfamo, Dean of Admissions, 609-652-4261

The Program
The Environmental Studies Program has been integral to Stockton's mission since the College's opening in 1971, partly due to Stockton's unique location within the New Jersey Pine Barrens, a superb environmental laboratory. The program offers both B.A. and B.S. degrees. Students whose study of the environment is combined with work in the social sciences and humanities earn the B.A. The B.S. serves students who wish more technical and scientific specialization. Graduation requirements include core and intermediate courses in environmental studies, related science, the Environmental Studies Seminar, and senior thesis or internship.

MAJOR/CONCENTRATIONS
Environmental Studies
- Biological Resources
- Cultural Resources
- Earth Resources
- Pollution Management

Special Features
On-campus facilities include a cartography room, chemical and biological laboratories, a greenhouse, biological and geological collections, and state-of-the-art geographic information systems. Approximately 400 acres of the 1,600-acre campus have been set aside for an arboretum, forestry nursery, ecological succession plots, and a study preserve.

The Result
Graduates find employment with regulatory agencies at all levels of government, with other public agencies, and with private sector employers. Seventy-five percent of graduates find employment or enter graduate school within 6 months of graduation.

Who's Recruiting Who on Campus
Employers: New Jersey Department of Environmental Protection and Energy, the New Jersey Pinelands Commission, Handex Corporation, Atlantic Electric, New Jersey Health Department, U.S. Environmental Protection Agency. **Positions:** Environmental Scientist, Conservationist, Wetlands Specialist.

UNIVERSITY OF CALIFORNIA, IRVINE
School of Social Ecology
Department of Environmental Analysis and Design
Irvine, California

Fast Facts About the Program
- **Established:** 1970
- **Enrollment:** 1,300
- **Faculty:** 60 (48 FT, 12 PT)
- **Student/Faculty Ratio:** 22:1
- **Degrees Conferred Since Inception:** 4,000
- **Degrees Conferred in 1991:** 400
- **Contact:** Dr. Daniel Stokols, Dean, School of Social Ecology, University of California, Irvine, Irvine, CA 92717; phone 714-856-6094

Fast Facts About the School
- State-supported coed university
- 1,489-acre campus in suburban setting
- **Enrollment:** 16,949
- **Faculty:** 743
- **Tuition:** State resident: $0; nonresident: $7699
- **Fees:** $2524
- **Room and Board:** $4993
- **Application Deadline:** Rolling
- **Entrance Difficulty Level:** Very difficult
- **Contact:** Dr. James Dunning, Director of Admissions, 714-856-6701

The Program
The Program in Social Ecology at the University of California, Irvine (UCI) was established in 1970 as an interdisciplinary academic unit spanning the environmental, legal, behavioral, and health sciences. The discipline of social ecology applies scientific methods to the study of a wide range of recurring social and environmental problems.

MAJOR/CONCENTRATIONS
Social Ecology
- Criminology, Law, and Society
- Environmental Analysis and Design
- Psychology and Social Behavior

Among issues of long-standing interest are crime and justice in society, social influences on human development over the life cycle, and effects of the physical environment on health and behavior. The program maintains a central interest in human adaptation and an interest in the study of events in the natural settings in which they occur. The multidisciplinary faculty includes psychologists, sociologists, criminologists, urban and regional planners, and environmental health scientists.

Special Features
The Social Ecology Building features several facilities for experimental research, including behavioral assessment laboratories for research in human development, health psychology, social relations, and legal studies; an environmental simulation laboratory for investigating the effects of varying environmental conditions on group performance; and wet laboratories for research and teaching in the environmental health sciences. The environmental simulation laboratory permits full-scale, realistic simulations of interior environments. An important aspect of the undergraduate program is its upper-division field study requirement for majors.

The Result
Students find jobs in planning departments, mental health settings, educational institutions, and many community and governmental agencies. They apply to graduate and professional schools of law, administration, public health, social welfare, psychology, sociology, criminology, and urban planning. Seventy-five to 80% of graduates find employment or enroll in graduate school within 6 months of graduation.

UNIVERSITY OF NORTH CAROLINA AT WILMINGTON

Environmental Studies
Wilmington, North Carolina

Fast Facts About the Program
- **Established:** 1973
- **Enrollment:** 148
- **Faculty:** 50 (all PT)
- **Student/Faculty Ratio:** 3:1
- **Degrees Conferred Since Inception:** 150–200
- **Degrees Conferred in 1991:** 23
- **Contact:** Wm. David Webster, Coordinator, Environmental Studies Program, 601 S. College Road, University of North Carolina at Wilmington, Wilmington, NC 28403-3297; phone 919-395-3487

Fast Facts About the School
- State-supported comprehensive coed institution
- 650-acre campus in urban setting
- **Enrollment:** 8,090
- **Faculty:** 409
- **Student/Faculty Ratio:** 16:1
- **Tuition:** State resident: $676; nonresident: $5730
- **Fees:** $626
- **Room and Board:** $3310
- **Application Deadline:** 2/15
- **Entrance Difficulty Level:** Moderately difficult
- **Contact:** Diane M. Zeeman, Director, Undergraduate Admissions, 919-395-3243

The Program
The Environmental Studies Program emphasizes the importance of a multidisciplinary approach in the study of environmental problems, particularly those dealing with the marine environment. The

> **MAJOR**
> Environmental Studies

curriculum exposes students to a broad range of analytical procedures in the natural and social sciences and has an area of specialization consisting of advanced course work in the biological, chemical, and earth sciences.

Special Features
The program uses the Center for Marine Science Research, which is located at Wrightsville Beach, 6 miles from the main campus. The center maintains 8 research vessels, ranging from 13 to 22 feet, and specialized equipment that includes a Superphantom Remotely Operated Vehicle. The center serves as host to the National Undersea Research Center, a facility sponsored by the National Oceanic and Atmospheric Administration (NOAA), which serves the southeastern United States. International student exchange programs are sponsored by UNCW's Office of International Programs and promote the exchange of ideas crucial to the development of global awareness.

Who's Recruiting Who on Campus
Employers: U.S. Army Corps of Engineers; U.S. Fish and Wildlife Service; North Carolina Wildlife Resources Commission; North Carolina Department of Health, Environment, and Natural Resources; North Carolina Division of Marine Fisheries; North Carolina Division of Coastal Management; E. I. Du Pont De Nemours and Company; General Electric

UNIVERSITY OF PENNSYLVANIA
Environmental Studies
Philadelphia, Pennsylvania

Fast Facts About the Program
- **Established:** 1971
- **Enrollment:** 45
- **Faculty:** 65 (62 FT, 3 PT)
- **Degrees Conferred Since Inception:** 250
- **Degrees Conferred in 1991:** 12
- **Contact:** Robert Giegengack, Professor of Geology and Director of the Undergraduate Major in Environmental Studies, Department of Geology, University of Pennsylvania, Philadelphia, PA 19104-6316; phone 215-898-5191

Fast Facts About the School
- Independent coed university
- 260-acre campus in urban setting
- **Enrollment:** 22,220
- **Faculty:** 4,152
- **Student/Faculty Ratio:** 7:1
- **Tuition:** $23,168
- **Fees:** $1640
- **Room and Board:** $6330
- **Application Deadline:** 1/1
- **Entrance Difficulty Level:** Most difficult
- **Contact:** Willis J. Stetson Jr., Dean of Admissions, 215-898-7502

The Program
The mission of environmental studies at the University of Pennsylvania is to offer a broad spectrum of academic opportunities, in addition to a flexible major curriculum, to enable students committed to

> **MAJOR**
> Environmental Studies

the study of the environment to qualify for challenging graduate programs or to find satisfying employment in the arena of environmental analysis.

Special Features
The University maintains an ambitious study-abroad program, within which environmental studies has special arrangements with programs at the Universities of Edinburgh and Ibadan, Nigeria. Students in environmental studies attend off-campus programs at the Sea Education Association in Woods Hole, Massachusetts; at sea aboard one of the Association's 2 sail-powered oceanographic research vessels; at the Yellowstone-Bighorn Research Association in Red Lodge, Montana; and at a variety of national and state parks, forest preserves, and wildlife refuges. Students may receive academic credit for participation in these programs and in other selected off-campus activities.

The Result
Half of the graduates in environmental studies choose to pursue advanced degrees. The other half who seek employment immediately after graduation find jobs in the EPA, other government agencies, environmental consulting firms, law firms, and research foundations. Many firms visit the campus via the University-wide Career Planning and Placement Service. Most environmental studies graduates who seek employment immediately upon finishing the program are placed through departmental contacts.

UNIVERSITY OF VERMONT
The Environmental Program
Burlington, Vermont

Fast Facts About the Program
- **Established:** 1972
- **Enrollment:** 600
- **Faculty:** 9 (7 FT, 2 PT)
- **Student/Faculty Ratio:** 67:1
- **Degrees Conferred Since Inception:** 1,100
- **Degrees Conferred in 1991:** 92
- **Contact:** Dr. Carl Reidel, Program Director, University of Vermont, 153 S. Prospect Street, Burlington, VT 05401; phone 802-656-4055

Fast Facts About the School
- State-supported coed university
- 425-acre campus in small-town setting
- **Enrollment:** 9,492
- **Faculty:** 1,017
- **Student/Faculty Ratio:** 15:1
- **Tuition:** State resident: $5314; nonresident: $13,914
- **Fees:** $414
- **Room and Board:** $4142
- **Application Deadline:** 2/1
- **Entrance Difficulty Level:** Moderately difficult
- **Contact:** Carol Hogan, Director of Admissions, 802-656-3370

The Program
The Environmental Program, the only University-wide academic program, offers students a major or minor in environmental studies within the College of Arts and Sciences, the College of Agriculture and Life Sciences, the School of Natural Resources, and the College of Education and Social Services.

MAJORS

Environmental Studies
Environmental Studies/Secondary Education

Requirements for the B.A. and B.S. are the completion of 120 semester hours, including a 6-credit senior research thesis and an individually designed component of upper-level courses. A semester abroad and community internships are highly recommended.

Special Features
The program maintains a diverse statewide system of natural areas, and a research vessel on Lake Champlain and several field centers offer unique study and research opportunities. Study-abroad programs are available through the School for International Training in Brattleboro, Vermont, and a variety of other programs. A majority of students take advantage of these programs to receive full credit toward their major. The Environmental Studies Enrichment Fund supports undergraduate conferences, speaker series, career workshops, and individual student grants for research and travel. Students also have a variety of internship opportunities.

The Result
Eighty to 90% of graduates find employment or enroll in graduate school within 6 months of graduation. Students attend graduate school within a wide range of science and humanities disciplines. Alumni work as journalists, teachers, and managers in public and private organizations. A significant number of graduates–perhaps the highest per capita in the United States–enter the Peace Corps upon graduation.

UTAH STATE UNIVERSITY
Department of Geography and Earth Resources
Logan, Utah

Fast Facts About the Program
- **Established:** 1988
- **Enrollment:** 64
- **Faculty:** 12 (all FT)
- **Student/Faculty Ratio:** 5:1
- **Degrees Conferred Since Inception:** 28
- **Degrees Conferred in 1991:** 10
- **Environmental Library:** Yes
- **Contact:** Derrick J. Thom, Head, Department of Geography and Earth Resources, College of Natural Resources, Utah State University, Logan, UT 84322-5240; phone 801-750-1790

Fast Facts About the School
- State-supported coed university
- 332-acre campus in urban setting
- **Enrollment:** 16,440
- **Faculty:** 970
- **Student/Faculty Ratio:** 20:1
- **Tuition:** State resident: $1686; nonresident: $4668
- **Room and Board:** $2507
- **Application Deadline:** 9/1
- **Entrance Difficulty Level:** Moderately difficult
- **Contact:** Mr. Lynn J. Poulsen, Assistant Vice-President, Student Affairs, 801-750-1107

The Program
Geography is the study of the relationship between human society and the physical environment. Students taking a major within the Department of Geography and Earth Resources are required to complete a set of core courses aimed at providing a general understanding of the physical, biological, and human dimensions of the earth and the interaction among these dimensions. Students are then encouraged to pursue advanced courses in a concentration. Students interested in fields of emphasis are advised to take predetermined courses to complete their emphasis.

MAJOR/CONCENTRATIONS
Geography
Ecology
Geographic Education
Geographic Information Systems
Human Geography
Physical Geography
Remote Sensing
Rural Development

Special Features
Surrounded by the Wasatch Range of the Rocky Mountains, Cache Valley provides a spectacular setting for education and environmental research. The USU campus is located on a bench created by ancient Lake Bonneville, overlooking Cache Valley. The department actively participates in the College of Natural Resources activities, including a field camp in the Wasatch National Forest and student exchange programs in Morocco, Mexico, and Iceland. Seminar series on natural resources management and environmental issues are sponsored by the College.

The Result
Cartographers, geographers, and remote sensing specialists are hired by the private sector. In the public sector, geographers may work for local and state economic development offices, conduct research on recreation and park utilization, or map land use from remotely sensed data. At the federal level, geographers most often work for the Defense Mapping Agency, the National Oceanic and Atmospheric Administration, the Forest Service, the U.S. Geological Survey, NASA, the Department of State, and the U.S. Census Bureau.

UTAH STATE UNIVERSITY
Environmental Studies
Logan, Utah

Fast Facts About the Program
- **Established:** 1970
- **Enrollment:** 80
- **Faculty:** 20 (18 FT, 2 PT)
- **Student/Faculty Ratio:** 4:1
- **Degrees Conferred Since Inception:** 480
- **Degrees Conferred in 1991:** 15
- **Environmental Library Holdings:** 5,000 bound volumes; 3,000 titles on microform; 100 periodical subscriptions
- **Contact:** Dr. Charles C. Grier, Department Head, College of Natural Resources, Utah State University, Logan, UT 84322-5215; phone 801-750-2455

Fast Facts About the School
- State-supported coed university
- 332-acre campus in urban setting
- **Enrollment:** 16,440
- **Faculty:** 970
- **Student/Faculty Ratio:** 20:1
- **Tuition:** State resident: $1686; nonresident: $4668
- **Room and Board:** $2507
- **Application Deadline:** 9/1
- **Entrance Difficulty Level:** Moderately difficult
- **Contact:** Mr. Lynn J. Poulsen, Assistant Vice-President, Student Affairs, 801-750-1107

The Program
Utah State seeks to provide students with a broad, multiresource, multidisciplinary education in the planning, management, and use of world environments. Students acquire an integrated understanding of the biological, physical, socioeconomic, and political sciences from a theoretical and practical

> **MAJORS**
> Environmental Analysis
> Environmental Education
> Environmental Management

perspective. The University provides students with a solid scientific foundation and practical fieldwork and summer employment. In their junior and senior years, students select a specialty that expands their qualifications. The University offers about 50 scholarships.

Special Features
All majors may attend a 6-week summer field camp at a 7,000-foot elevation in the Wasatch-Cache National Forest. For 25 years, all camp graduates have had paid summer jobs following the program, usually with federal agencies such as the U.S. Forest Service or National Park Service. Formal student exchanges are available with the major natural resource and environmental universities in Mexico, Morocco, and Iceland.

The Result
Graduates are employed by public and private organizations to perform a wide variety of activities, with about 47% accepting entry-level positions within 6 months of graduation. Another 28% immediately pursue graduate study. All graduates meet federal Office of Personnel Management requirements for soil conservationist or biologist.

Who's Recruiting Who on Campus
Employers: U.S. State Department, National Park Service, Bureau of Land Management, Peace Corps, U.S. Fish and Wildlife Service, U.S. Forest Service, state natural resource and fish/wildlife agencies, environmental consulting and management companies

WARREN WILSON COLLEGE
Environmental Studies Department
Swannanoa, North Carolina

Fast Facts About the Program
- **Established:** 1977
- **Enrollment:** 78
- **Faculty:** 8 (7 FT, 1 PT)
- **Student/Faculty Ratio:** 10:1
- **Degrees Conferred Since Inception:** 130
- **Degrees Conferred in 1991:** 15
- **Contact:** Woodward S. Bousquet, Department Chair, Environmental Studies, Warren Wilson College, 701 Warren Wilson Road, Swannanoa, NC 28778; phone 704-298-3325

Fast Facts About the School
- Independent comprehensive coed institution affiliated with Presbyterian Church (U.S.A.)
- 1,100-acre campus in small-town setting
- **Enrollment:** 560
- **Faculty:** 70
- **Student/Faculty Ratio:** 11:1
- **Tuition:** $8700
- **Fees:** $615
- **Room and Board:** $2852
- **Application Deadline:** Rolling
- **Entrance Difficulty Level:** Moderately difficult
- **Contact:** Thomas Weede, Dean of Admissions, 800-934-3536 Ext. 246

The Program
The environmental studies major began at Warren Wilson College in 1977 and has grown steadily to become the largest major at the College. The program combines courses in the natural and social sciences with fieldwork and internship options in rural, urban, and natural settings. Academic study is strengthened and supplemented by the College's on-campus work program and service learning program, both of which provide firsthand experience related to environmental studies. Through the work program, each resident student earns a fellowship of about $2000 for expenses.

MAJOR/CONCENTRATIONS
Environmental Studies
Environmental Analysis
Environmental Education
Environmental Policy
Forest Resource Conservation
Plant Biology and Horticulture
Wildlife Biology
Self-designed

Special Features
Warren Wilson's 1,100-acre campus encompasses a farm, an organic garden, mountain-slope forests, streams, and a river. Located in the heart of the Blue Ridge Mountains, the campus is near other educational resources that include the city of Asheville, Blue Ridge Parkway, 2 national forests, and the Great Smoky Mountains National Park. Opportunities for extended off-campus study include month-long trips to wilderness areas and appropriate technology projects in third-world countries. All students work 15 hours a week in the College's work program. Student work crews related to the Environmental Studies Department are in charge of the College's farm, garden, and science labs and landscaping, recycling, and community environmental outreach programs. Each student also performs at least 20 hours of community service annually.

The Result
Eighty percent of graduates find jobs in their field or enroll in graduate school within 6 months of graduation. Typical employers include government agencies, private forestry corporations, citizen groups, consulting firms, and environmental education centers.

Natural Resources Management

Natural resource management programs prepare professionals for careers that focus on the conservation of specific types of natural resources, including wildlife, freshwater and ocean fisheries, forests, rangeland, wilderness preserves, parks, and other outdoor recreational facilities.

BALL STATE UNIVERSITY
Natural Resources
Muncie, Indiana

Fast Facts About the Program
- **Established:** 1969
- **Enrollment:** 196
- **Faculty:** 9 (8 FT, 1 PT)
- **Student/Faculty Ratio:** 22:1
- **Degrees Conferred Since Inception:** 694
- **Degrees Conferred in 1991:** 21
- **Environmental Library:** Yes
- **Contact:** Dr. John Pichtel, Chair, Department of Natural Resources, Ball State University, Muncie, IN 47306; phone 317-285-5781

Fast Facts About the School
- State-supported coed university
- 955-acre campus in urban setting
- **Enrollment:** 20,488
- **Faculty:** 1,168
- **Student/Faculty Ratio:** 17:1
- **Tuition:** State resident: $2280; nonresident: $5360
- **Room and Board:** $2970
- **Application Deadline:** 3/1
- **Entrance Difficulty Level:** Moderately difficult
- **Contact:** Ruth Vedvik, Director of Admissions, 317-285-8287

The Program
The department prepares students for careers in environmental science and natural resources. The programs are designed to give students a basic scientific and socioeconomic understanding of ecosystems. The department also offers a minor in natural resources, a teaching minor in conservation and environmental studies, and an endorsement for elementary education majors and coordinates an interdepartmental energy minor.

MAJOR/CONCENTRATIONS
Natural Resources
  Environmental Protection
  Interpretation and Public Information
  Land Resource Management
  Natural Resources Studies
  Outdoor Recreation Management

Special Features
University-owned properties near the campus (e.g., the Ball State Wildlife Preserve) serve as laboratories for teaching and independent research. Other areas emphasize teaching and interpretation of natural resources. Each summer the department sponsors field courses; past field courses have studied resource management in Central America, Europe, Canada, the American West, and Appalachia. Internships and co-ops are offered by local, state, and federal agencies as well as by private consulting firms and environmental organizations.

The Result
Graduates pursue careers in local, state, and federal environmental and public health agencies; public and private utilities; industrial corporations; consulting firms; natural resource agencies; and outdoor recreation enterprises. About 60% of graduates find a job in their field or continue their studies within 6 months of graduation.

Who's Recruiting Who on Campus
Employers: U.S. Office of Surface Mining, Indiana Department of Environmental Management, Indiana Department of Natural Resources

CALIFORNIA POLYTECHNIC STATE UNIVERSITY, SAN LUIS OBISPO

Forestry and Natural Resources

San Luis Obispo, California

Fast Facts About the Program
- **Established:** 1968
- **Enrollment:** 347
- **Faculty:** 11 (7 FT, 4 PT)
- **Student/Faculty Ratio:** 32:1
- **Degrees Conferred Since Inception:** 600
- **Degrees Conferred in 1991:** 28
- **Contact:** Dr. Norman H. Pillsbury, Department Head, Natural Resources Management Department, California Polytechnic State University, San Luis Obispo, San Luis Obispo, CA 93407; phone 805-756-2702

Fast Facts About the School
- State-supported comprehensive coed institution
- 5,000-acre campus in small-town setting
- **Enrollment:** 17,758
- **Faculty:** 1,069
- **Student/Faculty Ratio:** 16:1
- **Tuition:** State resident: $0; nonresident: $7380
- **Fees:** $1200
- **Room and Board:** $3991
- **Application Deadline:** 11/30
- **Entrance Difficulty Level:** Very difficult
- **Contact:** Dr. Roger Swanson, Associate Vice President, Enrollment and Support Services, 805-756-1521

The Program
The program consists of special areas of study in environmental management, fire and chaparral management, hardwood management, parks and forest recreation, urban forestry, and watershed management.

Special Features
Special facilities include a plant and water lab with seed germination and cold storage chambers, a greenhouse, and a weather station. Also available

MAJOR/CONCENTRATIONS

Forestry and Natural Resources
Environmental Management
Fish and Wildlife Management
Forest Management
Parks and Forest Recreation
Urban Forestry
Watershed, Chapparral, and Fire
Management

are a tree farm, an energy plantation, a watershed, a reservoir, and various other field labs. Program students are offered opportunities to participate in career workshops twice a year. Seminar series are offered every 2 years as well. Study abroad in 6 countries is also available. The University has cooperative programs with the U.S. Forest Service, the Bureau of Land Management, the California Department of Forestry, and various city and county governments.

The Result
There are no unemployed graduates who actively sought work in their field. The school receives hundreds of job announcements each year from throughout the world.

Who's Recruiting Who on Campus
Employers: U.S. Forest Service, Bureau of Land Management, Environmental Care, California Department of Forestry and Fire Protection, Environmental Science. **Positions:** Timber Forester, Environmental Consultant, Soil Scientist, Urban Forester, Fire Resource Manager

CLEMSON UNIVERSITY
Aquaculture, Fisheries, and Wildlife Department
Clemson, South Carolina

Fast Facts About the Program	Fast Facts About the School
• **Established:** 1953	• State-supported coed university
• **Enrollment:** 140	• 1,400-acre campus in small-town setting
• **Faculty:** 8 (all FT)	• **Enrollment:** 17,295
• **Student/Faculty Ratio:** 18:1	• **Faculty:** 1,060
• **Degrees Conferred Since Inception:** 400	• **Student/Faculty Ratio:** 19:1
• **Degrees Conferred in 1991:** 8	• **Tuition:** State resident: $2460; nonresident: $6858
• **Contact:** D. Lamar Robinette, Department Head, Room G08, Lehotsky Hall, Clemson University, Clemson, SC 29634; phone 803-656-3117	• **Fees:** $170
	• **Room and Board:** $3100
	• **Application Deadline:** Rolling
	• **Entrance Difficulty Level:** Moderately difficult
	• **Contact:** Dr. Michael Heintze, Director of Admissions, 803-656-2287

The Program

Clemson University's Department of Aquaculture, Fisheries, and Wildlife (AFW) dates back to the 1930s. In 1984 a separate department was formed as the result of a cooperative research and public service program begun by the University and the South Carolina Wildlife and Marine Resources Department. Today, the department offers Bachelor of Science and Master of Science degrees in

MAJOR/CONCENTRATIONS

Aquaculture, Fisheries, and Wildlife
Aquaculture
Fisheries
Preveterinary
Wildlife
Wildlife Toxicology

aquaculture, fisheries, and wildlife biology. Programs of study emphasize relationships between wild animals and their changing environments as well as the production of aquatic organisms. Over the past 2 years, the department and associated programs have more than doubled and continue to grow.

Special Features

The Archbold Tropical Research Center (ATRC) is a consortium of institutions that includes several major universities, the National Park Service, the U.S. Forest Service, and the Smithsonian Institution. ATRC has a field research station on the West Indies island of Dominica that includes 5 major buildings and several smaller ones that provide a total of 30,000 square feet of floor space. The station is on approximately 230 acres of land that are available for research on tropical ecology, agroforestry, and tropical agriculture. The Delta Atlantic Flyway Substation in Georgetown, South Carolina, facilitates research on wintering waterfowl and wetland management in South Carolina's coastal wetlands for students, faculty, and state biologists.

The Result

Students who earn the bachelor's degree typically pursue graduate studies in all areas of biological science and veterinary medicine. Seventy-five percent of graduates find employment or enroll in graduate school within 6 months of graduation. Career opportunities include work in the U.S. Department of Agriculture and state departments of natural resources, private wildlife management foundations, and pharmaceutical companies.

COLORADO STATE UNIVERSITY
Natural Resources Management
Fort Collins, Colorado

Fast Facts About the Program
- **Established:** 1971
- **Enrollment:** 157
- **Faculty:** 14 (all FT)
- **Student/Faculty Ratio:** 11:1
- **Degrees Conferred Since Inception:** 240
- **Degrees Conferred in 1991:** 18
- **Contact:** Karen Dirks, Department Secretary, Department of Forest Sciences, Colorado State University, Fort Collins, CO 80523; phone 303-491-6911

Fast Facts About the School
- State-supported coed university
- 833-acre campus in urban setting
- **Enrollment:** 20,967
- **Faculty:** 1,019
- **Student/Faculty Ratio:** 20:1
- **Tuition:** State resident: $1855; nonresident: $6558
- **Fees:** $507
- **Room and Board:** $3624
- **Application Deadline:** 7/1
- **Entrance Difficulty Level:** Very difficult
- **Contact:** Mary Ontiveros, Director of Admissions, 303-491-6909

The Program
The major is designed to give students a background in the concepts and practices of natural resources management. The approach is broad in order to include all resource aspects, but it is also

> **MAJOR**
> Natural Resources Management

structured to ensure that students develop a solid basis for professional careers. Students select a minor from a choice of more than 50 areas available in the University. A total of 128 credits is required for graduation. Of these, 45 credits must be at the 300 level or above. A 4-week summer natural resources camp and 1 season of full-time employment in natural resource work are also required.

Special Features
Students complete a summer field program between their sophomore and junior years at the Pingree Park mountain campus. This facility is located 55 miles west of Fort Collins and is surrounded by the Roosevelt National Forest, adjacent to Rocky Mountain National Park. Students may be selected for cooperative education programs by federal natural resource agencies, or they may wish to work in an internship program with private companies, nonprofit organizations, local government offices, or state agencies. Study-abroad programs are available for a semester's work in New Zealand, Scotland, and Mexico. Students typically gain experience in their field by working, during the summer, for natural resource organizations.

The Result
An estimated 66% of graduates find employment or enroll in graduate school within 6 months of graduation. Graduates are employed in such diverse fields as international forestry, environmental consulting, computer technology, youth agency administration, mining reclamation, surveying, land use planning, park management, real estate management, community forestry, integrated pest management, nature conservation, natural resource communications, and public relations. Some graduates pursue graduate work in environmental law or a specialized resource area needed in consulting.

COLORADO STATE UNIVERSITY
Recreation Resource Management
Fort Collins, Colorado

Fast Facts About the Program
- **Established:** 1960
- **Enrollment:** 318
- **Faculty:** 22 (18 FT, 4 PT)
- **Student/Faculty Ratio:** 14:1
- **Degrees Conferred Since Inception:** 1,200
- **Degrees Conferred in 1991:** 60
- **Environmental Library Holdings:** 200 bound volumes; 8 periodical subscriptions
- **Contact:** Dr. Glenn Haas, Chairman, Department of Recreation Resources, College of Natural Resources, Colorado State University, Fort Collins, CO 80523; phone 303-491-5126

Fast Facts About the School
- State-supported coed university
- 833-acre campus in urban setting
- **Enrollment:** 20,967
- **Faculty:** 1,019
- **Student/Faculty Ratio:** 20:1
- **Tuition:** State resident: $1855; nonresident: $6558
- **Fees:** $507
- **Room and Board:** $3624
- **Application Deadline:** 7/1
- **Entrance Difficulty Level:** Very difficult
- **Contact:** Mary Ontiveros, Director of Admissions, 303-491-6909

The Program
Colorado State has one of the largest academic programs in the world that focuses on natural-resource-based recreation. The University's recreation resources department offers nationally accredited undergraduate programs; a nationally respected graduate research program in the applied and basic

> **MAJOR/CONCENTRATIONS**
> **Recreation Resource Management**
> Commercial Recreation and Tourism
> Park and Recreation Administration
> Resource Interpretation

social sciences; and professional service to public land agencies and rural communities. The department's mission is to help students steward the Earth's natural resources and assist in the sustained production of goods and the management of services. Students specialize their program through a concentration. The park and recreation administration concentration helps students develop expertise in managing public recreation resources and providing quality recreation experiences to visitors. Students taking the commercial recreation and tourism concentration develop expertise in operating private commercial recreation and tourism enterprises and in providing quality recreation experiences to their customers. Students who take the resource interpretation concentration acquire expertise in developing and managing public education programs related to the Earth's natural environment.

The Result
Sixty percent of graduates find employment in their field or enroll in graduate school within 6 months of graduation.

Who's Recruiting Who on Campus
Employers: U.S. Forest Service, Bureau of Land Management, National Park Service, Colorado State Park Service, Colorado Tourism Board, Wilderness Society, Ecotourism Society, private tourism companies

---

EASTERN NEW MEXICO UNIVERSITY
B.S. in Wildlife Management
Portales, New Mexico

Fast Facts About the Program
- **Established:** 1972
- **Enrollment:** 50
- **Faculty:** 6 (all FT)
- **Student/Faculty Ratio:** 8:1
- **Degrees Conferred Since Inception:** 30
- **Degrees Conferred in 1991:** 5
- **Contact:** Dr. A. L. Gennaro, Professor, Department of Biology, Eastern New Mexico University, Portales, NM 88130; phone 505-562-2723

Fast Facts About the School
- State-supported comprehensive coed institution
- 240-acre campus in small-town setting
- **Enrollment:** 3,879
- **Faculty:** 200
- **Student/Faculty Ratio:** 22:1
- **Tuition:** State resident: $864; nonresident: $4422
- **Fees:** $492
- **Room and Board:** $2430
- **Application Deadline:** Rolling
- **Entrance Difficulty Level:** Minimally difficult
- **Contact:** Larry Fuqua, Director of Admissions, 505-562-2178 or 800-367-3668

The Program

The program provides students with an expertise in management of the aquatic and terrestrial biota and prepares them for employment with private, state, and federal agencies. This degree has been

MAJOR
Wildlife Management

especially popular because of the availability of natural outdoor laboratories in the complete array of life zones. Classroom, laboratory, and field courses deal with aquatic and terrestrial plants, invertebrates, and vertebrates.

Special Features

The program is supported by a large Natural History Biotic Collection of aquatic and terrestrial plants, insects, fishes, amphibians, reptiles, birds, and mammals, as well as by the outdoor Natural History Prairie Preserve, which has not been grazed by domestic livestock for over 50 years. The University has cooperative agreements with the U.S. Fish and Wildlife Service, Bureau of Land Management, New Mexico Department of Game and Fish, and U.S. Forest Service. Through these agreements, these agencies provide summer and regular school term employment.

The Result

About 75% of graduates find a job in their field or go on to advanced study within 6 months of graduation.

Who's Recruiting Who on Campus

Employers: U.S. Fish and Wildlife Service, National Park Service, New Mexico Department of Game and Fish, U.S. Forest Service, New Mexico Environmental Improvement Division.
Positions: Wildlife Officers, Rangers, Refuge Managers, Research Biologists, Environmental Inspectors.

LONG ISLAND UNIVERSITY, SOUTHAMPTON CAMPUS

Marine Science
Southampton, New York

Fast Facts About the Program
- **Established:** 1965
- **Enrollment:** 276
- **Faculty:** 24 (20 FT, 4 PT)
- **Student/Faculty Ratio:** 12:1
- **Degrees Conferred Since Inception:** 973
- **Degrees Conferred in 1991:** 28
- **Contact:** Carol Gilbert, Director of Admissions, Long Island University, Southampton Campus, Southampton, NY 11968; phone 516-283-4000 Ext. 200

Fast Facts About the School
- Independent comprehensive coed institution
- 110-acre campus in rural setting
- **Enrollment:** 1,458
- **Faculty:** 120
- **Student/Faculty Ratio:** 18:1
- **Tuition:** $9540
- **Fees:** $510
- **Room and Board:** $5060
- **Application Deadline:** Rolling
- **Entrance Difficulty Level:** Moderately difficult
- **Contact:** Carol Gilbert, Director of Admissions, 516-283-4000 Ext. 200

The Program
The purpose of the Marine Science Program is to educate students in the scientific aspects of the marine environment, with exposure to both freshwater and saltwater environments. The goal is to produce graduates who are competent in marine science by providing them with a solid background in one of 3 major disciplines: biology, chemistry, or geology. The program has produced 14 Fulbright scholarship winners in the past 17 years.

MAJOR/CONCENTRATIONS
Marine Science
Marine Biology
Marine Chemistry
Marine Geology

Special Features
Special features of the program include the campus location on Shinnecock Bay, minutes from the Atlantic Ocean; a Marine Station on campus; a fleet of research vessels; and aquaculture labs. Cooperative education and internships are available at EPCOT Center in Florida, Woods Hole in Massachusetts, the Smithsonian Institution, the Scripps Institute, and Brookhaven Laboratory. Study abroad through the Friends World Program is available at any of 7 overseas centers. The "Seamester" offers a semester aboard a 110-foot sailing schooner traveling the Atlantic coastline. Students may also study marine biology during a January travel course that goes to the South Pacific and Australia's Great Barrier Reef.

The Result
Most graduates go directly into career positions, although the acceptance rate at graduate school is 90%. Students typically become part of the staff at aquariums; local, state, and federal departments of the Environmental Conservation and Planning organization; environmental engineering firms; fish hatcheries; and aquaculture firms. They may also perform research at any National Oceanic and Atmospheric Administration site. Ninety-three percent of graduates find employment in their field or enter graduate school within 6 months of graduation. Eighty percent of students who do co-ops are offered permanent positions by their employers.

LOUISIANA TECH UNIVERSITY
School of Forestry
Ruston, Louisiana

Fast Facts About the Program
- **Established:** 1946
- **Enrollment:** 108
- **Faculty:** 11 (all FT)
- **Student/Faculty Ratio:** 10:1
- **Degrees Conferred Since Inception:** 1,039
- **Degrees Conferred in 1991:** 14
- **Contact:** G. H. Weaver, Director, School of Forestry, P.O. Box 10138 TS, Louisiana Tech University, Ruston, LA 71272; phone 318-257-4985

Fast Facts About the School
- State-supported coed university
- 235-acre campus in small-town setting
- **Enrollment:** 10,380
- **Faculty:** 427
- **Student/Faculty Ratio:** 23:1
- **Tuition:** State resident: $1841; nonresident: $2996
- **Room and Board:** $2115
- **Application Deadline:** Rolling
- **Entrance Difficulty Level:** Noncompetitive
- **Contact:** Karen Akin, Dean of Admissions, 318-257-3036

The Program
The goals of the programs of the School of Forestry include the undergraduate education of men and women in forestry and natural resources; conducting research activities that contribute to the attainment of regional economic, social, and environmental goals with regard to forest lands and associated resources; and enabling and encouraging students, faculty, and staff to advance the profession of forestry throughout the state, region, nation, and world.

MAJORS/CONCENTRATIONS

Forestry
Forest Business
Forest Management
Forest Recreation
Wildlife Management
Wood Utilization

Special Features
In the spring of 1984, a group of alumni and friends of the School of Forestry met to discuss ways of paying tribute to Professor Lloyd P. Blackwell, who was instrumental in the organization of the School of Forestry and served as chief administrator for the first 30 years. One of his greatest ambitions was to introduce forestry students to recognized leaders in the forestry profession. In order to achieve this goal, the decision was made to establish and permanently endow the Lloyd P. Blackwell Visiting Lectureship. The School of Forestry is housed on South Campus in three modern and well-organized buildings. Other facilities on the South Campus include a renovated sawmill, a storage building, and a greenhouse complex. A summer camp facility is located at Corney Lake, 30 miles north of campus. The forestry faculty recognizes the importance of having a well-managed forest property for long-term faculty research and student education.

The Result
School of Forestry graduates have built a record of accomplishment in their professional careers. Leadership roles include regional vice president for a major forest industry and state leadership positions with public agencies.

Who's Recruiting Who on Campus
Employers: Champion International, Willamette Industries, International Paper Co., Stone Container Corp., state and federal agencies

NEW MEXICO STATE UNIVERSITY
Fishery and Wildlife Sciences
Las Cruces, New Mexico

Fast Facts About the Program
- **Established:** 1985
- **Enrollment:** 161
- **Faculty:** 6 (all FT)
- **Student/Faculty Ratio:** 27:1
- **Degrees Conferred Since Inception:** 200
- **Degrees Conferred in 1991:** 20
- **Contact:** Dr. Paul Turner, Assistant Professor, Fishery and Wildlife Sciences, New Mexico State University, Las Cruces, NM 88003; phone 505-646-1707

Fast Facts About the School
- State-supported coed university
- 5,800-acre campus in suburban setting
- **Enrollment:** 15,334
- **Faculty:** 802
- **Student/Faculty Ratio:** 19:1
- **Tuition:** State resident: $1594; nonresident: $5290
- **Fees:** $18
- **Room and Board:** $2544
- **Application Deadline:** 8/14
- **Entrance Difficulty Level:** Moderately difficult
- **Contact:** Bill J. Bruner, Director of Admissions, 505-646-3121

The Program

The Department of Fishery and Wildlife Sciences seeks to disseminate information on the ecology and management of wild animals and their habitats through classroom teaching, scientific writing, and public contact.

Special Features

Facilities include 2 University ranches for research, the nearby Jornada Experimental Range with ongoing long-term ecological research, the San Andres National Wildlife Refuge, Dripping Springs Natural Area, Aquirre Springs Recreational Area, White Sands National Monument, and Organ Mountains Wilderness Study Area.

The Result

Bachelor of Science graduates work as conservation officers, fish and wildlife biologists, wildlife refuge managers, and range and soil conservationists with state and federal agencies. Some graduates work for game ranches, zoos, consulting firms, and universities. Ninety percent of graduates find employment or enroll in graduate school within 6 months of graduation.

MAJORS/CONCENTRATIONS

Fishery Science
Aquaculture
Fishery Management
Fishery Research
Water Quality

Wildlife Science
General Wildlife Management
Rangeland Wildlife Management
Wildlife Damage Control
Wildlife Research

Options Common to Both Majors
Endangered Species Management
Fishery and Wildlife Administration
Fishery and Wildlife Communications
Fishery and Wildlife Law Enforcement
Interpretive Natural History

Who's Recruiting Who on Campus

Employers (Positions): U.S. Fish and Wildlife Service (Wildlife Refuge Manager, Fisheries Biologist, Wildlife Biologist); U.S. Forest Service (Fisheries Biologist, Wildlife Biologist); U.S. Bureau of Land Management (Bureau of Land Management Ranger, Wildlife Biologist); U.S. Department of Agriculture Animal and Plant Inspection Service (Wildlife Biologist)

OKLAHOMA STATE UNIVERSITY
Forestry
Stillwater, Oklahoma

Fast Facts About the Program
- **Established:** 1946
- **Enrollment:** 55
- **Faculty:** 11 (all FT)
- **Student/Faculty Ratio:** 5:1
- **Degrees Conferred Since Inception:** 1,075
- **Degrees Conferred in 1991:** 6
- **Contact:** Dr. Edwin L. Miller, Department Head, Department of Forestry, 008C AG Hall, Oklahoma State University, Stillwater, OK 74078; phone 405-744-5438

Fast Facts About the School
- State-supported coed university
- 900-acre campus in small-town setting
- **Enrollment:** 19,476
- **Faculty:** 691
- **Student/Faculty Ratio:** 22:1
- **Tuition:** State resident: $1395 to $1488; nonresident: $4495 to $4983
- **Fees:** $373
- **Room and Board:** $3008
- **Application Deadline:** Rolling
- **Entrance Difficulty Level:** Moderately difficult
- **Contact:** Dr. Robin Lacy, Registrar and Director of Admissions, 405-744-6876

The Program

The Department of Forestry offers a major in forestry leading to a Bachelor of Science degree in agriculture. Course work in forest management is offered for the individual with career aspirations in the U.S. Forest Service and other federal agencies, state and local forestry organizations, the forest industry, and consulting. Courses in forest products are designed for those interested in the business, manufacturing, and sales aspects of forestry. For the student with a research career in mind, course work in forest science is available.

MAJOR/CONCENTRATIONS

Forestry
Forest Management
Forest Products
Forest Science

Special Features

Requirements for a Bachelor of Science degree include the successful completion of a 9-week summer camp and a total of 140 credit hours of course work. The summer camp is scheduled to follow the sophomore year and is held annually in different forest settings. The Department of Forestry maintains two research stations in southeastern Oklahoma in the midst of the Quachita National Forest. Field trips to this area comprise part of the instruction in many forestry courses.

The Result

Eighty percent of graduates find employment or pursue graduate study within 6 months of graduation. Graduates with a Bachelor of Science degree may be employed by federal agencies, including the U.S. Forest Service, Bureau of Land Management, the Soil Conservation Service, the Fish and Wildlife Service, and the Bureau of Indian Affairs. In addition, state, county and municipal governments employ foresters in a variety of positions. Wood-using industries retain foresters for land management, land and timber acquisition, and harvesting positions as well as in mill production and administrative work. Foresters work for associations promoting the use of forest products and in many other public relations jobs. Some foresters are self-employed as consultants, specializing in timber and land appraisals, management planning, and a variety of special services.

OKLAHOMA STATE UNIVERSITY
Wildlife and Fisheries Ecology
Stillwater, Oklahoma

Fast Facts About the Program
- **Established:** 1945
- **Enrollment:** 87
- **Faculty:** 8 (all FT)
- **Student/Faculty Ratio:** 11:1
- **Degrees Conferred in 1991:** 13
- **Contact:** Dr. Jerry Wilhm, Department Head, Zoology, 430 Life Sciences West, Oklahoma State University, Stillwater, OK 74078; phone 405-744-5555

Fast Facts About the School
- State-supported coed university
- 900-acre campus in small-town setting
- **Enrollment:** 19,476
- **Faculty:** 691
- **Student/Faculty Ratio:** 22:1
- **Tuition:** State resident: $1395 to $1488; nonresident: $4495 to $4983
- **Fees:** $373
- **Room and Board:** $3008
- **Application Deadline:** Rolling
- **Entrance Difficulty Level:** Moderately difficult
- **Contact:** Dr. Robin Lacy, Registrar and Director of Admissions, 405-744-6876

The Program
The wildlife and fisheries ecology undergraduate program involves comprehensive study in the conservation of renewable natural resources with an emphasis on the optimum balance between wild animal populations and habitat requirements. Courses in the wildlife and fisheries program fulfill the requirements for many other applied and professional careers, including preparation for graduate programs.

MAJOR/CONCENTRATIONS
Wildlife and Fisheries Ecology
Communications
Fisheries
Management/Research

Special Features
Undergraduates majoring in wildlife and fisheries ecology may choose from communications, fisheries, and management/research concentrations. In communications, biological training is combined with course work in journalism, social sciences, and the uses of electronic media. Management/research emphasizes applied wildlife and fisheries ecology and offers the best preparation for graduate study. The department includes a water quality laboratory and a cooperative fisheries and wildlife research unit.

The Result
A wide choice of careers is open to the wildlife and fisheries ecology graduate. Careers include manager of game and nongame species and natural areas, researcher, administrator, information specialist, educator, veterinarian, lawyer, naturalist, and consultant. A host of graduate programs provide opportunities in forestry, agronomy, biology, ecology, zoology, environmental science, wildlife and fisheries science, and natural resource management. Fifty to 60% of graduates find employment or enroll in graduate school within 6 months of graduation.

THE PENNSYLVANIA STATE UNIVERSITY
Forest Products
University Park, Pennsylvania

Fast Facts About the Program
- **Established:** 1942
- **Enrollment:** 13
- **Faculty:** 4 (all FT)
- **Student/Faculty Ratio:** 3:1
- **Degrees Conferred Since Inception:** 431
- **Degrees Conferred in 1991:** 4
- **Contact:** Ellen A. Manno, Coordinator, Undergraduate Program, Pennsylvania State University, 213 Ferguson Building, University Park, PA 16802; phone 814-863-0362

Fast Facts About the School
- State related coed university
- 5,013-acre campus in small-town setting
- **Enrollment:** 38,989
- **Faculty:** 2,177
- **Student/Faculty Ratio:** 19:1
- **Tuition:** State resident: $4332; nonresident $9118
- **Fees:** $70
- **Room and Board:** $3670
- **Application Deadline:** Rolling
- **Entrance Difficulty Level:** Very difficult
- **Contact:** Director of Undergraduate Admissions, 814-865-5478

The Program
The mission of the Program is to effectively transfer scientific and technological information about the utilization and conversion of the timber resource base into useful products for society. For the Bachelor of Science degree in forest products, a minimum of 129 credits is required.

MAJOR/CONCENTRATIONS
Forest Products
  Management
  Science

Special Features
A wood shop and pilot circular sawmill on campus are used for research and for resident education as are several pieces of specialized equipment used in wood mechanics and wood composite evaluation. A forest resources field orientation course allows students to visit forest resources and wood products industries statewide. On-campus recruiting is conducted by an average of 4 to 8 employers annually. An active student chapter of the Forest Products Research Society sponsors guest speakers and involves students in projects related to their major.

The Result
Ninety percent of graduates find employment in their field or enroll in graduate school within 6 months of graduation. Employment includes a mix of opportunities in production, engineering, and sales. Students seek positions as quality control technicians, process technicians, quality assurance technicians, production managers, market research supervisors, salesmen, research assistants, and technical service representatives.

Who's Recruiting Who on Campus
Employers (Positions): International Paper Company (Process Technician); Temple Inland Forest Products Corporation (Process Technician–summer internship); Mann and Parker Lumber (Sales); Rex Lumber Company (Sales); Bailey Lumber Company (Technical Service Representative); National Caesin (Technical Service Representative); Nestle Corporation (Technical Service Representative); Trus Joist MacMillan (Technical Service Representative)

THE PENNSYLVANIA STATE UNIVERSITY
Forest Science
University Park, Pennsylvania

Fast Facts About the Program
- **Established:** 1907
- **Enrollment:** 105
- **Faculty:** 11 (all FT)
- **Student/Faculty Ratio:** 10:1
- **Degrees Conferred Since Inception:** 3,618
- **Degrees Conferred in 1991:** 15
- **Contact:** Ellen A. Manno, Coordinator, Undergraduate Programs, Pennsylvania State University, 213 Ferguson Building, University Park, PA 16802; phone 814-863-0362

Fast Facts About the School
- State related coed university
- 5,013-acre campus in small-town setting
- **Enrollment:** 38,989
- **Faculty:** 2,177
- **Student/Faculty Ratio:** 19:1
- **Tuition:** State resident: $4332; nonresident $9118
- **Fees:** $70
- **Room and Board:** $3670
- **Application Deadline:** Rolling
- **Entrance Difficulty Level:** Very difficult
- **Contact:** Director of Undergraduate Admissions, 814-865-5478

The Program
The mission of the program is to impart an understanding of the science and technology needed in managing forest ecosystems and to provide the basic education necessary for the development of

> **MAJOR**
> Forest Science

individuals as responsible members of society. For the Bachelor of Science degree in forest science, a minimum of 132 credits is required. A forest science minor is also offered.

Special Features
The School of Forest Resources manages a 6,900-acre experimental forest 15 miles from the University Park Campus. Vast areas of state forest land and some state game lands are also nearby. Greenhouses and experimental plantings on or near campus are used in certain courses. A forest resources field orientation course gives students the opportunity to visit forest resources and wood products industries statewide. On-campus recruiting for seasonal positions is conducted by an average of 3 to 5 employers annually. An active student forestry society sponsors guest speakers and involves students in projects related to their majors.

The Result
Within a year of graduation, 60% to 80% of graduates are employed in professional positions and an additional 5% to 20% are in graduate school. About half of all employment opportunities are in the public sector, and half are in the private sector. Positions students apply for include forester, procurement forester, forestry technician, biological technician, field technician, research technician, sales and service technician, and arborist.

Who's Recruiting Who on Campus
Employers (Positions): Appleton Papers (Industrial Forest Consultant–summer internship); Chesapeake Corporation (Forestry Student Aid); International Paper Company (Summer Field Forester and Forester); Coastal Lumber Company (Summer Forest Technician); Ecology and Environment (Environmental Consultants); Peace Corps (Forestry Volunteer); Student Conservation Association (volunteers)

THE PENNSYLVANIA STATE UNIVERSITY
Wildlife and Fisheries Science
University Park, Pennsylvania

Fast Facts About the Program
- **Established:** 1981
- **Enrollment:** 180
- **Faculty:** 4 (all FT)
- **Student/Faculty Ratio:** 45:1
- **Degrees Conferred Since Inception:** 227
- **Degrees Conferred in 1991:** 26
- **Contact:** Ellen A. Manno, Coordinator, Undergraduate Programs, Pennsylvania State University, 213 Ferguson Building, University Park, PA 16802; phone 814-863-0362

Fast Facts About the School
- State related coed university
- 5,013-acre campus in small-town setting
- **Enrollment:** 38,989
- **Faculty:** 2,177
- **Student/Faculty Ratio:** 19:1
- **Tuition:** State resident: $4332; nonresident $9118
- **Fees:** $70
- **Room and Board:** $3670
- **Application Deadline:** Rolling
- **Entrance Difficulty Level:** Very difficult
- **Contact:** Director of Undergraduate Admissions, 814-865-5478

The Program
The mission of the Wildlife and Fisheries Science Program is to provide a challenging and comprehensive curriculum in concepts, principles, and techniques of wildlife and fisheries science and nat-

> **MAJOR**
> Wildlife and Fisheries Science

ural resource conservation and management. For the Bachelor of Science degree, a minimum of 132 credits is required. A wildlife and fisheries science minor is also offered.

Special Features
The School of Forest Resources manages a 6,900-acre experimental forest 15 miles from the University Park Campus. This experimental forest and other university-owned woodlands are used in the program. Vast areas of state forest land and some state game lands are also nearby and provide additional sites for field instruction. Bird, mammal, and fish collections maintained on or near campus are used in undergraduate courses. A 20-acre deer pen, used primarily for research and public education, provides some work-study opportunities for undergraduates. An active student chapter of the Wildlife Society sponsors guest speakers and involves students in projects related to their major.

The Result
Within a year of graduation, 60% to 80% of graduates are employed in professional positions, and an additional 5% to 20% go on to graduate school. The majority of employment opportunities are in the public sector. Positions for which students apply include wildlife biologist, biological technician, field technician, research technician, lab technician, information specialist, zoo naturalist, zoological assistant, and environmental scientist.

Who's Recruiting Who on Campus
Employers (Positions): National Park Service (Biological Technician–seasonal position); U.S. Forest Service (Biological Technician–seasonal position); Ecology and Environment (Environmental Consultant); Peace Corps (volunteers); Student Conservation Association (volunteers in many natural resource areas)

STOCKTON STATE COLLEGE
Marine Science
Pomona, New Jersey

Fast Facts About the Program
- **Established:** 1973
- **Enrollment:** 178
- **Faculty:** 5 (all FT)
- **Student/Faculty Ratio:** 36:1
- **Degrees Conferred Since Inception:** 481
- **Degrees Conferred in 1991:** 30
- **Contact:** Richard Hager, Marine Science Program Coordinator, Natural Sciences and Mathematics Department, Stockton State College, Pomona, NJ 08240; phone 609-652-4546

Fast Facts About the School
- State-supported 4-year coed college
- 1,600-acre campus in small-town setting
- **Enrollment:** 4,965
- **Faculty:** 288
- **Student/Faculty Ratio:** 17:1
- **Tuition:** State resident: $1984; nonresident: $3096
- **Fees:** $472
- **Room and Board:** $3840
- **Application Deadline:** 5/1
- **Entrance Difficulty Level:** Very difficult
- **Contact:** Salvatore Catalfamo, Dean of Admissions, 609-652-4261

The Program
Stockton is one of few institutions offering an undergraduate degree program in marine science. This is a flagship program at Stockton because of the College's proximity to marine environments and their importance to New Jersey. The program emphasizes applied studies in marine resources management and aquaculture and seeks to actively involve students in research.

MAJORS/CONCENTRATIONS
Marine Biology
  Marine Biology
  Marine Resource Management
Oceanography
  Marine Geology
  Physical/Chemical Oceanography

Special Features
Many marine habitats are available for field projects, including beaches, pilings, and breakwaters; eroding peat deposits; bays with mud and shell bottoms; salt marsh ponds, creeks, and grass flats; and low-salinity creeks and rivers forming the upper reaches of estuaries. Stockton has a fleet of small boats, with sampling gear for field courses and research activity and the *R.V. Luce*, a 33-foot oceangoing vessel. Interns have been placed locally in field and laboratory positions. Through the Washington Internship program, students have been placed at the National Aquarium, the National Academy of Sciences, and the Natural History Museum of the Smithsonian Institution. Stockton is a member of the New Jersey Marine Sciences Consortium (NJMSC) and has access to the consortium's marine station, boats, and equipment.

The Result
Stockton graduates in marine biology have obtained entry-level positions in local, state, and federal agencies, including laboratory work, fieldwork on marine habitats, data analysis, and regulation or consulting work in private firms. Oceanography and marine geology students work as water chemists, physical oceanographers, and marine biologists. Seventy-six percent of graduates find employment or enroll in graduate school within 6 months of graduation.

UNITY COLLEGE
Conservation Law Enforcement
Unity, Maine

Fast Facts About the Program
- **Established:** 1978
- **Enrollment:** 122
- **Faculty:** 61 (33 FT, 28 PT)
- **Student/Faculty Ratio:** 2:1
- **Degrees Conferred Since Inception:** 572
- **Degrees Conferred in 1991:** 86
- **Contact:** Dr. John M. B. Craig, Vice-President, Dean for Admissions, Unity College, Unity, ME 04988; phone 207-948-3131 Ext. 222

Fast Facts About the School
- Independent 4-year coed college
- 185-acre campus in rural setting
- **Enrollment:** 417
- **Faculty:** 57
- **Student/Faculty Ratio:** 14:1
- **Tuition:** State resident: $7400; nonresident: $8500
- **Room and Board:** $4525
- **Application Deadline:** Rolling
- **Entrance Difficulty Level:** Moderately difficult
- **Contact:** Dr. John M. B. Craig, Vice-President, Dean for Admissions, 207-948-3131 Ext. 222

The Program
The Conservation Law Enforcement Program at Unity College, which leads to a Bachelor of Science in Environmental Sciences degree, integrates a firm foundation in law enforcement with preparation in wildlife and fisheries management. Because the conservation officer's primary duty is to protect nat-

MAJOR/CONCENTRATIONS
Conservation Law Enforcement
Fisheries
Park Management
Wildlife

ural resources, the program provides students with a strong natural science background. Students learn about trees, fish, birds, and mammals. They study habits and habitats and investigate the scientific principles on which natural resource management is based.

Special Features
Unity's internship program gives students the chance to work directly with professionals in the field. Through this program, students can earn college credit while gaining valuable job-related experience.

The Result
Conservation law enforcement is a demanding profession that requires great dedication. Irregular hours, poor weather conditions, and occasional hazardous duty are all part of the conservation officer's life. Physical stamina and good health are important. In spite of these disadvantages, the field is extremely competitive. All students find employment or enroll in graduate school within 6 months of graduation.

Who's Recruiting Who on Campus
Employers (Positions): Maine Warden Service (Game Warden); New Hampshire Department of Fish and Game (Conservation Officer); Connecticut Department of Environmental Protection (Conservation Officer); U.S. Fish and Wildlife Service (Special Agent, Wildlife Inspector); U.S. Customs Service (Border Patrol Agent); Baxter State Park (Park Ranger); Maine State Police (State Trooper)

UNITY COLLEGE
Park Management
Unity, Maine

Fast Facts About the Program
- **Established:** 1979
- **Enrollment:** 38
- **Faculty:** 61 (33 FT, 28 PT)
- **Degrees Conferred Since Inception:** 162
- **Degrees Conferred in 1991:** 12
- **Contact:** Dr. John M. B. Craig, Vice-President, Dean for Admissions, Unity College, P.O. Box 532, Unity, ME 04988; phone 207-948-3131 Ext. 222

Fast Facts About the School
- Independent 4-year coed college
- 185-acre campus in rural setting
- **Enrollment:** 417
- **Faculty:** 57
- **Student/Faculty Ratio:** 14:1
- **Tuition:** State resident: $7400; nonresident: $8500
- **Room and Board:** $4525
- **Application Deadline:** Rolling
- **Entrance Difficulty Level:** Moderately difficult
- **Contact:** Dr. John M. B. Craig, Vice-President, Dean for Admissions, 207-948-3131 Ext. 222

The Program
The Park Management Program at Unity College provides the broad-based preparation a student needs to be an effective park manager. The park manager is a generalist with a firm academic background in environmental, social, and administrative

> **MAJOR/CONCENTRATION**
>
> **Park Management**
> Environmental Education

sciences. Courses range from firearms training to plant and animal identification to program administration. The program leads to a Bachelor of Science in social science degree. In addition to both classroom and laboratory-based courses and fieldwork, many Unity students choose to participate in an internship as part of their academic program.

Special Features
The Cooperative Education Program at Unity College enriches a student's education by integrating work experience with academic study. Field experience gives students the chance to explore career opportunities, to test career choices, and to further develop skills in their chosen field. Unity graduates have a competitive edge in the job market because they are better trained, more confident, and have established professional contacts through their cooperative education experiences. To meet the needs of more adventurous students, Unity College offers a variety of opportunities in Europe and Africa.

The Result
Unity College graduates are employed in park management positions in local, state, and federal parks throughout the United States. Locations include Acadia National Park in Maine, Bandelier National Monument in New Mexico, Battleship Cove Historic Park in Massachusetts, Baxter State Park in Maine, the Frye Mountain Management Area in Maine, the George Washington Management Area in Rhode Island, the Maine Warden Service in Maine, the Massachusetts State Park Systems, and the Ruffingham Wildlife Management Area in Maine. All graduates find employment or enroll in graduate school within 6 months of graduation.

UNITY COLLEGE
Wilderness-Based Outdoor Recreation
Unity, Maine

Fast Facts About the Program	**Fast Facts About the School**
• **Established:** 1976 • **Enrollment:** 67 • **Faculty:** 61 (33 FT, 28 PT) • **Student/Faculty Ratio:** 1:1 • **Degrees Conferred Since Inception:** 201 • **Degrees Conferred in 1991:** 28 • **Contact:** Dr. John M. B. Craig, Vice-President, Dean for Admissions, Unity College, P.O. Box 532, Unity, ME 04988; phone 207-948-3131 Ext. 222	• Independent 4-year coed college • 185-acre campus in rural setting • **Enrollment:** 417 • **Faculty:** 57 • **Student/Faculty Ratio:** 14:1 • **Tuition:** State resident: $7400; nonresident: $8500 • **Room and Board:** $4525 • **Application Deadline:** Rolling • **Entrance Difficulty Level:** Moderately difficult • **Contact:** Dr. John M. B. Craig, Vice-President, Dean for Admissions, 207-948-3131 Ext. 222

The Program

The Unity College Outdoor Wilderness Recreation Program is unique. Focusing on wilderness-based outdoor recreation leadership, the curriculum blends professional education in natural resource management with the study of the arts and humani-

> **MAJOR/CONCENTRATIONS**
>
> **Wilderness-Based Outdoor Recreation**
> Outdoor Administration
> Outdoor Leadership

ties. The major purpose of the concentrations in outdoor administration and outdoor leadership is to prepare a thoroughly skilled professional who will have several options in developing his or her career.

Special Features

The Cooperative Education Program at Unity College enriches a student's education by integrating work experience with academic study. Field experiences give students the chance to explore career opportunities, to test career choices, and to further develop skills in their chosen field. Unity graduates have a competitive edge in the job market because of their cooperative education experience. Unity College offers a variety of opportunities in Europe and Africa.

The Result

Outdoor recreation/education positions have been plentiful nationwide for baccalaureate degree holders during the past decade, and the outlook is for continued growth. Graduates have become wilderness instructors, operators and managers of tourism enterprises, teachers, and park rangers as well as therapeutic recreation specialists. Some students choose to pursue a graduate degree. All students find employment or enroll in graduate school within 6 months of graduation.

Who's Recruiting Who on Campus

Employers (Positions): Outward Bound in Florida (Logistic Supervisor, Program Director for Project STEP); Hurricane Island Outward Bound School (Chief Climbing Instructor); Arizona State University (Recreation Sports Director)

UNITY COLLEGE
Wildlife
Unity, Maine

Fast Facts About the Program
- **Established:** 1978
- **Enrollment:** 48
- **Faculty:** 61 (33 FT, 28 PT)
- **Degrees Conferred Since Inception:** 174
- **Degrees Conferred in 1991:** 14
- **Contact:** Dr. John M. B. Craig, Vice-President, Dean for Admissions, Unity College, P.O. Box 532, Unity, ME 04988; phone 207-948-3131 Ext. 222

Fast Facts About the School
- Independent 4-year coed college
- 185-acre campus in rural setting
- **Enrollment:** 417
- **Faculty:** 57
- **Student/Faculty Ratio:** 14:1
- **Tuition:** State resident: $7400; nonresident: $8500
- **Room and Board:** $4525
- **Application Deadline:** Rolling
- **Entrance Difficulty Level:** Moderately difficult
- **Contact:** Dr. John M. B. Craig, Vice-President, Dean for Admissions, 207-948-3131 Ext. 222

The Program
The Wildlife Program at Unity College prepares students for entry-level positions, especially with government agencies. The curriculum includes a broad selection of classes in biology and general science. Wildlife courses emphasize identification of

MAJOR/CONCENTRATION
Wildlife
  Ecology

species, natural history, and principles of wildlife management. Students are strongly encouraged to gain practical experience by completing an internship. The program meets or exceeds the Wildlife Society's certification requirements.

Special Features
Unity's rural setting is a key benefit for wildlife majors who use the area's forests, fields, lakes, and streams as natural laboratories. Bangor and Augusta are each less than an hour's drive from Unity, and this proximity promotes close working relationships with public and private wildlife organizations in these cities. The Cooperative Education Program enriches a student's education by integrating work experience with academic study. Participation allows students to earn college credit for work experience and gain a competitive edge in the job market.

The Result
Wildlife biologists can choose from a variety of career opportunitites in wildlife management, research, or administration. Government agencies, such as the U.S. Fish and Wildlife Service, the U.S. Forest Service, and the National Park Service, provide numerous opportunities. Private-sector employers include the National Wildlife Federation, the Audubon Society, game farms, and consulting firms. Virtually all graduates find employment or enroll in graduate school within 6 months of graduation.

Who's Recruiting Who on Campus
Employers: Bureau of Indian Affairs, Bureau of Land Management, Environmental Protection Agency, Moosehorn National Wildlife Refuge, Massachusetts Department of Fisheries and Wildlife, Pennsylvania Game Commission, Philadelphia Zoo

UNIVERSITY OF ALASKA FAIRBANKS
Natural Resources Management
Fairbanks, Alaska

Fast Facts About the Program
- **Established:** 1976
- **Enrollment:** 77
- **Faculty:** 25 (all FT)
- **Student/Faculty Ratio:** 3:1
- **Degrees Conferred Since Inception:** 180
- **Degrees Conferred in 1991:** 13
- **Contact:** Barbara J. Pierson, Student Affairs Coordinator, School of Agriculture and Land Resources Management, University of Alaska Fairbanks, Fairbanks, AL 99775; phone 907-474-5276

Fast Facts About the School
- State-supported coed university
- 2,250-acre campus in small-town setting
- **Enrollment:** 4,664
- **Faculty:** 711
- **Student/Faculty Ratio:** 14:1
- **Tuition:** State resident: $1320; nonresident: $3960
- **Fees:** $550
- **Room and Board:** $3100
- **Application Deadline:** 8/1
- **Entrance Difficulty Level:** Moderately difficult
- **Contact:** James T. Mansfield, Associate Director, Admissions and Records, 907-474-7521

The Program
The Natural Resources Management program teaches students to make and implement decisions to develop, maintain, and protect ecosystems. The Bachelor of Science degree, requiring 130 semester hours, is designed for students desiring careers in resources management or planning advanced study.

MAJOR/CONCENTRATIONS
Natural Resources Management
Forestry
Plant, Animal, and Soil Science
Resources

Three options are available: forestry; plant, animal, and soil science; and resources.

Special Features
Research disciplines range from soil, animal, and food science; forestry; horticulture; land planning to resource law and policy. Summer internships are available in designated state and federal agencies. Student exchange programs include universities in Europe, Canada, Venezuela, Mexico, Japan, and the United States.

The Result
Ninety-five percent of graduates find employment or enroll in graduate school within 6 months of graduation. Graduates are employed in professional resource management positions in Canada, Alaska, and other states in the U.S. They are working as recreation and environmental planners, foresters, park rangers, soil conservationists, environmental assessment officers, and interpretive specialists.

Who's Recruiting Who on Campus
Employers (Positions): Bureau of Land Management (Recreation Specialist, Natural Resource Interpreter); National Park Service (Park Ranger, Interpretive Services); Alaska Department of Natural Resources (Forest Technician, Land Planner); U.S. Fish and Wildlife Service (Habitat Specialist)

UNIVERSITY OF MAINE
Natural Resources
Orono, Maine

Fast Facts About the Program
- **Established:** 1960
- **Enrollment:** 100
- **Faculty:** 25 (all FT)
- **Student/Faculty Ratio:** 4:1
- **Degrees Conferred Since Inception:** 500 to 1,000
- **Degrees Conferred in 1991:** 15
- **Contact:** Mark W. Anderson, Coordinator, Natural Resources Program, Winslow Hall, University of Maine, Orono, ME 04469; phone 207-581-3228

Fast Facts About the School
- State-supported coed university
- 3,298-acre campus in small-town setting
- **Enrollment:** 12,804
- **Faculty:** 769
- **Tuition:** State resident: $2310; nonresident: $6540
- **Fees:** $408
- **Room and Board:** $4241
- **Application Deadline:** 2/1
- **Entrance Difficulty Level:** Moderately difficult
- **Contact:** William J. Munsey, Director of Admissions, 207-581-1561

The Program
The Natural Resources Program is an interdisciplinary, science-based program designed to prepare students for careers in environmental protection and in management and conservation of natural resources. Students earn a Bachelor of Science degree with 120 course credits.

Special Features
Students participate in research projects with program faculty members. Students also may pursue internships and have field experience during the summer and can study abroad during their junior year. An annual speakers series brings outside experts to the University campus.

The Result
Sixty-five percent of graduates find employment in

MAJOR/CONCENTRATIONS

Natural Resources
Earth Sciences
Environmental Entomology
Environmental History and Social Science Perspectives
Environmental Sciences
Government and Public Policy
Land-Use Planning
Marine Resources and Sciences
Natural History and Ecology
Resource and Environmental Economics
Soil and Water Conservation
Waste Management
Students may select an individualized concentration as well.

their field or enroll in graduate school within 6 months of graduation. Recent graduates are working as soil scientists with environmental consulting firms, environmental entomologists, environmental technicians for manufacturing firms, policy analysts for state agencies, research associates in federal ecology labs, and environmental specialists with federal agencies. Recent graduates have pursued graduate degrees in resource economics, plant biology, soil science, and aquaculture.

Who's Recruiting Who on Campus
Employers (Positions): National Oceanic and Atmospheric Administration (Office Trainee); Envirologic Data (Environmental Research Analyst); Somerset County Environmental Education Center (Naturalist); U.S. Environmental Protection Agency (Environmental Biologist); Rizzo Association (Project Environmental Scientist); U.S. Bureau of Land Management (Analytical Wildlife Biologist)

UNIVERSITY OF MICHIGAN
School of Natural Resources
Ann Arbor, Michigan

Fast Facts About the Program	Fast Facts About the School
• **Established:** 1880	• State-supported coed university
• **Enrollment:** 300	• 2,607-acre campus in suburban setting
• **Faculty:** 28 (all FT)	• **Enrollment:** 36,228
• **Student/Faculty Ratio:** 11:1	• **Faculty:** 3,310
• **Degrees Conferred Since Inception:** 4,500	• **Student/Faculty Ratio:** 7:1
• **Degrees Conferred in 1991:** 90	• **Tuition:** State resident: $3710 to $4602; nonresident: $12,818 to $14,312
• **Contact:** Director of Academic Programs, University of Michigan, School of Natural Resources, Room 1024, 430 E. University, Ann Arbor, MI 48109-1115; phone 313-764-6453	• **Fees:** $135
	• **Room and Board:** $4084
	• **Application Deadline:** 2/1
	• **Entrance Difficulty Level:** Very difficult
	• **Contact:** Richard H. Shaw Jr., Director, Undergraduate Admissions, 313-764-7433

The Program

The study of natural resources and environmental problems has been a part of the University of Michigan for over 100 years. In 1950, the University established the School of Natural Resources, the first school of its kind in the world. Today, the School of Natural Resources (SNR) remains an international

> **MAJORS**
>
> **Environmental Policy and Behavior**
> **Landscape Design and Planning**
> **Resource Ecology and Management**

leader in educating and training students to become innovative and effective environmental managers, scientists, policymakers, and advocates.

Special Features

SNR freshman and sophomore students have the opportunity to participate in the school's highly innovative mentoring program. This program pairs undergraduates with graduate student mentors who have similar academic interests. Juniors and seniors have the opportunity to participate in the junior/senior mentoring program that matches students with environmental professionals in the Ann Arbor area. At the University's Biological Station located in northern Michigan, field courses in ecology, mammology, natural resource planning and management, and ornithology are taught. SNR students have many opportunities to study abroad for a summer, a semester, or a year. SNR has a formal exchange program with the University of Waterloo in Canada and belongs to a consortium of schools offering a program in sustainable development and tropical ecology in Costa Rica. With assistance from SNR's Office of Academic Programs, Career Planning and Placement Service, and Career Resource Center, students find a wide range of employment opportunities in the public, private, and nonprofit sectors.

Who's Recruiting Who on Campus

Employers (Positions): Alaska Sea Grant (Public Information Specialist); Philadelphia Zoo (Education Coordinator); Ohio Department of Natural Resources (Staff Forester); Ecology and Environment, Inc. (Environmental Consultant); Illinois Natural Resources Inventory (Aquatic Ecologist); U.S. Fish and Wildlife Service (Wildlife Biologist); U.S. Environmental Protection Agency (Environmental Scientist)

UNIVERSITY OF MISSOURI–COLUMBIA
Fisheries and Wildlife
Columbia, Missouri

Fast Facts About the Program
- **Established:** 1937
- **Enrollment:** 173
- **Faculty:** 8
- **Student/Faculty Ratio:** 22:1
- **Degrees Conferred Since Inception:** 423
- **Degrees Conferred in 1991:** 26
- **Contact:** Dr. William Kurtz, Director, Undergraduate Studies, 1-74 Agriculture Building, University of Missouri–Columbia, Columbia, MO 65211; phone 314-882-4567

Fast Facts About the School
- State-supported coed university
- 1,335-acre campus in small-town setting
- **Enrollment:** 24,660
- **Faculty:** 1,804
- **Tuition:** State resident: $2442 to $3282; nonresident: $7302 to $8142
- **Fees:** $370
- **Room and Board:** $3160
- **Application Deadline:** 5/15
- **Entrance Difficulty Level:** Moderately difficult
- **Contact:** Georgeanne Porter, Director, Undergraduate Admissions, 314-882-7786

The Program
The University's Fisheries and Wildlife Program has been developed to instill in students the concepts, skills, and ethics necessary for the study, management, use, protection, and conservation of renewable natural resources. The curriculum is designed to provide students with a basic understanding of renewable natural resources, with specialization in forestry or fisheries and wildlife, and to help students develop skills that facilitate the application and expansion of this understanding as a graduate. Degree requirements include agriculture law, animal population dynamics and management, botany, chemistry, earth sciences, ecology, fisheries and wildlife, genetics, physics, physiology, plant taxonomy, and zoology. There are approximately 8 named scholarships for fisheries and wildlife majors.

MAJOR/CONCENTRATIONS
Fisheries and Wildlife
Fishery Management
Fishery Science
Urban Wildlife Management
Wildlife Management
Wildlife Science

Special Features
Special facilities include the Thomas S. Baskett Wildlife and Research Education Center; the Gaylord Memorial Laboratory; the University State Forest; the Cooperative Fisheries and Wildlife Research Unit; and the National Fisheries Contaminant Research Center, in conjunction with the Department of the Interior.

The Result
Students establish careers as fish biologists, fishery managers, hatchery managers, wildlife biologists, wildlife managers, conservation agents, water quality specialists, and park managers. Fifty-five to 60% of students find employment or enroll in graduate school within 6 months of graduation.

Who's Recruiting Who on Campus
Employers: Missouri Department of Conservation, Arkansas Parks Department, Forest Service, U.S. Department of the Interior, Missouri Department of Natural Resources, Peace Corps, Weyerhauser

UNIVERSITY OF MISSOURI–COLUMBIA
Forestry
Columbia, Missouri

Fast Facts About the Program
- **Established:** 1947
- **Enrollment:** 157
- **Faculty:** 10
- **Student/Faculty Ratio:** 16:1
- **Degrees Conferred Since Inception:** 466
- **Degrees Conferred in 1991:** 4
- **Contact:** Dr. William Kurtz, Director, Undergraduate Studies, 1-74 Agriculture Building, University of Missouri–Columbia, Columbia, MO 65211; phone 314-882-4567

Fast Facts About the School
- State-supported coed university
- 1,335-acre campus in a small-town setting
- **Enrollment:** 24,660
- **Faculty:** 1,804
- **Student/Faculty Ratio:** 14:1
- **Tuition:** State resident: $2442–$3282; nonresident: $7302–$8142
- **Room and Board:** $3160
- **Application Deadline:** 5/15
- **Entrance Difficulty Level:** Moderately difficult
- **Contact:** Georgeanne Porter, Director, Undergraduate Admissions, 314-882-7786

The Program
The Forestry Program at the University of Missouri–Columbia has been developed to instill in students the concepts, skills, and ethics necessary for the study, management, use protection, and conservation of renewable natural resources. Students in the program have as their goal the attainment of the Bachelor of Science degree. Degree requirements

MAJOR/CONCENTRATIONS
Forestry
Forestry Resource Management
Individualized Studies
Industrial Forest Management
Urban Forestry

include the completion of courses in botany, chemistry, ecology and renewable resource management, geology, natural resource policy/administration, physics, and resource measurement, including 20 hours of forestry classes. There are approximately 15 named scholarships and awards available exclusively for forestry majors.

Special Features
A cooperative areement has been made with the North Central Forest Experiment Station. Other facilities include the Hard Wood Management Research Project, the Thomas S. Baskett Wildlife and Research Education Center, the Gaylord Memorial Laboratory, and University State Forest.

The Result
There are career opportunities for students to work as foresters, silviculturalists, nursery managers, industrial foresters, urban foresters, park managers, timber buyers, and conservation agents. Between 75% and 80% of graduates find employment or enroll in graduate school within 6 months of graduation. The School of Natural Resources offers a Master of Science in Forestry degree and a Doctor of Philosophy in Forestry degree.

Who's Recruiting Who on Campus
Employers: U.S. Army Corp of Engineers, Osmose, the Missouri Department of Conservation, the Arkansas Parks Department, the USDA Forestry Service, the U.S. Department of the Interior, Weyerhauser

---

UNIVERSITY OF NEW HAMPSHIRE
Department of Natural Resources
Durham, New Hampshire

Fast Facts About the Program
- **Established:** 1945
- **Enrollment:** 350
- **Faculty:** 18 (all FT)
- **Student/Faculty Ratio:** 19:1
- **Degrees Conferred Since Inception:** 2,000 to 3,000
- **Degrees Conferred in 1991:** 75
- **Contact:** Bill Mautz, Chairman, Department of Natural Resources, University of New Hampshire, Durham, NH 03824; phone 603-862-1020

Fast Facts About the School
- State-supported coed university
- 200-acre campus in small-town setting
- **Enrollment:** 11,219
- **Faculty:** 825
- **Student/Faculty Ratio:** 17:1
- **Tuition:** State resident: $3290; nonresident: $9840
- **Fees:** $397
- **Room and Board:** $3600
- **Application Deadline:** 2/1
- **Entrance Difficulty Level:** Moderately difficult
- **Contact:** Stanwood C. Fish, Dean of Admissions, 603-862-1360

The Program

The Department of Natural Resources seeks to provide its students with the skills necessary to become future leaders in the stewardship of the earth's natural resources. The department comprises faculty members who represent a wide variety of environmental interests. Historically, the department has been multidisciplinary, and the faculty is committed

MAJORS

Environmental Conservation
Forestry
Soil Science
Water Resources Management
Wildlife

to an interdisciplinary approach; efforts are made to involve undergraduates from each of the majors in areas of common concern. In addition to gaining a quality education in a selected area of study, each student is exposed to, and interacts with, students and faculty members from each of the other programs.

Special Features

The department is ideally situated in terms of ecology, economics, sociology, and politics for the study of natural resources. New Hampshire is a predominantly forested, rural state with mountains, lakes, a seacoast, and an estuarine system in addition to a climate with 4 seasons. This location, which incorporates a diverse environment, development pressure from Boston, a range of political viewpoints, and a mixture of land ownership, provides students with a unique educational opportunity. Nearly 100 faculty and graduate student research projects provide sources for student involvement.

The Result

Fifty to 75% of graduates find employment or enroll in graduate school within 6 months of graduation. Students in forestry, soil science, water resources management, and wildlife generally find employment with the federal and state agencies most closely aligned with their discipline, or they find jobs with private consulting firms and nonprofit organizations. Of these specific majors, students within the soil major have the best employment prospects at the present time, followed closely by those within the water resources management major. Forestry and wildlife majors also have good job opportunities, although the high interest in the latter increases competition. The Department of Natural Resources maintains current files of pertinent job and graduate school opportunities.

UNIVERSITY OF VERMONT
Recreation Management
Burlington, Vermont

Fast Facts About the Program
- **Established:** 1970
- **Enrollment:** 80
- **Faculty:** 8 (5 FT, 3 PT)
- **Student/Faculty Ratio:** 10:1
- **Degrees Conferred in 1991:** 14
- **Contact:** Dr. Robert E. Monning, Chairman, School of Natural Resources, Aiken Center, University of Vermont, Burlington, VT 05445; phone 802-656-2684

Fast Facts About the School
- State-supported coed university
- 425-acre campus in small-town setting
- **Enrollment:** 9,492
- **Faculty:** 1,017
- **Student/Faculty Ratio:** 15:1
- **Tuition:** State resident: $5314; nonresident: $13,914
- **Fees:** $414
- **Room and Board:** $4142
- **Application Deadline:** 2/1
- **Entrance Difficulty Level:** Moderately difficult
- **Contact:** Carol Hogan, Director of Admissions, 802-656-3370

The Program

The Recreation Management Program, part of the School of Natural Resources, addresses the relationship between society and the natural environment within the broad context of recreation and leisure. It is ultimately concerned with the issue of how society might best make use of its natural resource base for recreation, tourism, and related purposes. The educational objectives of the program are twofold. First, students are offered a well-rounded liberal arts and sciences education to enhance their membership in, and contributions to, society. Second, students are prepared for a variety of career opportunities within the outdoor recreation and tourism fields.

MAJOR/CONCENTRATIONS

Recreation Management
Private Outdoor Recreation
Tourism

Special Features

Students are exposed to business and government representatives through scheduled seminars, field trips, and class presentations. Facilities used for field trips, class projects, and student research include the Green Mountain National Forest, Vermont state parks, and private ski areas. The program operates an active internship program that provides students with a variety of campus-based, summer-long, off-campus internships. Eleven separate University properties throughout the state are available for field instruction in forestry.

The Result

The park and outdoor recreation management option is designed for students with a professional interest in governmental natural resources and outdoor recreation agencies and related nonprofit organizations. The tourism, travel, and hospitality management option is designed for students with a professional interest in travel and hospitality industries and tourism-related enterprises. Approximately 60% of graduates find jobs in their field or enroll in graduate school within 6 months of graduation.

Who's Recruiting Who on Campus

Employers: Walt Disney World College Program; U.S. Army Corps of Engineers; Department of Forests, Parks, and Recreation; U.S. Forest Service

---

UTAH STATE UNIVERSITY
Fisheries and Wildlife
Logan, Utah

Fast Facts About the Program	Fast Facts About the School
• **Established:** 1946	• State-supported coed university
• **Enrollment:** 170	• 332-acre campus in urban setting
• **Faculty:** 15 (all FT)	• **Enrollment:** 16,440
• **Student/Faculty Ratio:** 11:1	• **Faculty:** 970
• **Degrees Conferred Since Inception:** 1,200	• **Student/Faculty Ratio:** 20:1
• **Degrees Conferred in 1991:** 16	• **Tuition:** State resident: $1686; nonresident: $4668
• **Contact:** Raymond D. Dueser, Department Head, Fisheries and Wildlife Department, Utah State University, Logan, UT 84322-5210; phone 801-750-2463	• **Room and Board:** $2507
	• **Application Deadline:** 9/1
	• **Entrance Difficulty Level:** Moderately difficult
	• **Contact:** Mr. Lynn J. Poulsen, Assistant Vice-President, Student Affairs, 801-750-1107

The Program
The department's philosophy is to promote a broad interdisciplinary approach to natural resource problems and management. Students begin by taking courses designed to give them an overview. Students then specialize in wildlife management or

> **MAJOR/CONCENTRATIONS**
>
> **Fisheries and Wildlife**
> Fisheries Management
> Wildlife Management

fisheries management. The wildlife management option includes courses that focus on using quantitative techniques in natural resource management and problem solving. The fisheries management option prepares students to deal with the development and biological functions of fish, the physical and chemical aspects of water environments, the techniques of fish sampling, and fishery management principles.

Special Features
The department collaborates with and is the headquarters for the Utah Cooperative Fish and Wildlife Research Unit, the USDA Predator Ecology and Behavior Project, and the USDA Forest Service Fish and Wildlife Habitats Relationships Program.

The Result
Employment is available with federal and state conservation agencies, private environmental consulting firms, private game farms, hunting and fishing preserves, refuges, and energy development firms. Graduates often work as wildlife management biologists, fisheries management biologists, conservation officers, and fish hatcheries biologists. With additional experience and education, graduates can pursue careers in management planning, systems analysis, and environmental or resource impact analyses. Seventy-five percent of graduates find employment in their field or go on to advanced study within 6 months of graduation.

Who's Recruiting Who on Campus
Employers: U.S. Fish and Wildlife Service, U.S. Forest Service, Bureau of Land Management, Bureau of Reclamation, U.S. Army Corps of Engineers, Bureau of Indian Affairs, National Marine Fisheries Service, National Parks Service

---

UTAH STATE UNIVERSITY
Forest Resources
Logan, Utah

Fast Facts About the Program
- **Established:** 1930
- **Enrollment:** 130
- **Faculty:** 21 (20 FT, 1 PT)
- **Student/Faculty Ratio:** 6:1
- **Degrees Conferred Since Inception:** 2,000
- **Degrees Conferred in 1991:** 20
- **Environmental Library Holdings:** 10,000 bound volumes; 2,000 titles on microform; 50 periodical subscriptions
- **Contact:** Dr. Charles Grier, Head, Forest Resources Department, Utah State University, Logan, UT 84332; phone 801-750-2455

Fast Facts About the School
- State-supported coed university
- 332-acre campus in urban setting
- **Enrollment:** 16,440
- **Faculty:** 970
- **Student/Faculty Ratio:** 20:1
- **Tuition:** State resident: $1686; nonresident: $4668
- **Room and Board:** $2507
- **Application Deadline:** 9/1
- **Entrance Difficulty Level:** Moderately difficult
- **Contact:** Mr. Lynn J. Poulsen, Assistant Vice-President, Student Affairs, 801-750-1107

The Program
Utah State provides students with a broad, multi-resource education in the planning, management, and use of forest environments. Students acquire an integrated understanding of the biological, physical, socioeconomic, and political sciences. The University provides students with a solid scientific foundation, along with practical fieldwork and summer employment, upon which students can select a specialty in their junior and senior years. The University offers about 50 scholarships to department students.

MAJORS/CONCENTRATIONS
Forest Resources Management
Computer Applications
Forest Ecology
Forest Management
Outdoor Recreation
Policy
Urban Forestry
Watershed Management
Self-designed Minor
Outdoor Recreation

Special Features
All majors attend a 6-week summer field camp in the Wasatch-Cache National Forest. All camp graduates have paid summer jobs following camp, usually with federal agencies. Formal student exchanges are arranged with universities in Mexico, Morocco, and Iceland.

The Result
Graduates are employed by public and private organizations throughout the world, with 50% of graduates finding a job in their field within 6 months of commencement. Another 20% pursue graduate degrees immediately. All graduates meet federal Office of Personnel Management requirements for the positions of forester, soil conservatist, and biologist.

Who's Recruiting Who on Campus
Employers: U.S. Forest Service, National Park Service, Bureau of Land Management, Peace Corps, U.S. Fish and Wildlife Service, state natural resource and fish/wildlife agencies, many environmental consulting companies

UTAH STATE UNIVERSITY
Range Science
Logan, Utah

Fast Facts About the Program
- **Established:** 1933
- **Enrollment:** 41
- **Faculty:** 8 (all FT)
- **Student/Faculty Ratio:** 5:1
- **Degrees Conferred Since Inception:** 1,000
- **Degrees Conferred in 1991:** 12
- **Environmental Library Holdings:** 550 bound volumes; 2 periodical subscriptions
- **Contact:** Dr. John Malechek, Professor, Department of Range Science, Utah State University, Logan, UT 84322-5230; phone 801-750-2471

Fast Facts About the School
- State-supported coed university
- 332-acre campus in urban setting
- **Enrollment:** 16,440
- **Faculty:** 970
- **Student/Faculty Ratio:** 20:1
- **Tuition:** State resident: $1686; nonresident: $4668
- **Room and Board:** $2507
- **Application Deadline:** 9/1
- **Entrance Difficulty Level:** Moderately difficult
- **Contact:** Mr. Lynn J. Poulsen, Assistant Vice-President, Student Affairs, 801-750-1107

The Program
This program's mission is to train people to manage natural rangeland resources for sustained use and to conduct research that addresses issues in natural resource management. Undergraduates must complete 198 quarter credit hours of course work, including field trips and a summer training camp. Several scholarships are available.

> **MAJOR/CONCENTRATIONS**
> **Range Science**
> Forest-Range Management
> Range Economics
> Rangeland Rehabilitation
> Range-Wildlife Relations
> Watershed Management
> Special Curriculum for a Career Overseas

Special Features
Utah State offers special features such as a satellite library in the College of Natural Resources, permanent field research stations that also serve as teaching facilities, and well-developed associated programs in wildlife management, forestry, and geography and remote sensing. Through the scholarship program, juniors have the opportunity to study at a collaborating institution in Mexico, Iceland, or Morocco. Undergraduates are encouraged to interact with graduate students and become engaged in a research project.

The Result
Graduates often pursue careers in natural resource management, particularly the management of public lands. Many accept range conservationist positions with government agencies. Advanced study is pursued in such fields as game range management, international range management, and range animal production. Ninety-five percent of graduates find a job in their field or go on to advanced study within 6 months of graduation.

Who's Recruiting Who on Campus
Employers: Students have been recruited by government agencies, including the U.S. Forest Service, Bureau of Land Management, Soil Conservation Service, and Department of Defense, and by private organizations such as Nature Conservancy. **Positions:** These employers are looking for Range Conservationists, Field Ecologists, and Natural Resource Managers.

UTAH STATE UNIVERSITY
Recreation Resources Management
Logan, Utah

Fast Facts About the Program
- **Established:** 1935
- **Enrollment:** 80
- **Faculty:** 20 (18 FT, 2 PT)
- **Student/Faculty Ratio:** 4:1
- **Degrees Conferred Since Inception:** 1,120
- **Degrees Conferred in 1991:** 15
- **Environmental Library Holdings:** 5,000 bound volumes; 2,000 titles on microform; 100 periodical subscriptions
- **Contact:** Dr. Charles C. Grier, Department Head, Forest Resources Department, Utah State University, Logan, UT 84322-5215; phone 801-750-2455

Fast Facts About the School
- State-supported coed university
- 332-acre campus in urban setting
- **Enrollment:** 16,440
- **Faculty:** 970
- **Student/Faculty Ratio:** 20:1
- **Tuition:** State resident: $1686; nonresident: $4668
- **Room and Board:** $2507
- **Application Deadline:** 9/1
- **Entrance Difficulty Level:** Moderately difficult
- **Contact:** Mr. Lynn J. Poulsen, Assistant Vice-President, Student Affairs, 801-750-1107

The Program
The University provides students with a broad, multiresource education in the planning, management, and use of outdoor recreation in wildland environments. Students acquire an integrated understand-

> **MAJOR**
> **Recreation Resources Management**

ing of the biological, physical, socioeconomic, and political sciences. Students are given a solid scientific foundation, along with practical fieldwork and summer employment, upon which they select a specialty in their junior and senior years. The University offers about 50 scholarships to department program participants.

Special Features
All majors attend a 6-week summer field camp in the Wasatch-Cache National Forest. All camp graduates have paid summer jobs following that program, usually with federal agencies. Formal student exchanges are available with universities in Mexico, Morocco, and Iceland.

The Result
Graduates are employed by public and private organizations throughout the world, with about 55% accepting jobs in their field within 6 months of graduation. Another 25% pursue advanced studies immediately after graduation. All graduates meet federal Office of Personnel Management requirements for the position of outdoor recreation planner, forester, soil conservationist, and biologist.

Who's Recruiting Who on Campus
Employers: The National Park Service, the Bureau of Land Management, Peace Corps, the U.S. Fish and Wildlife Service, the U.S. Forest Service, state natural resource and fish/wildlife agencies, private recreational firms (e.g., ski resorts), environmental consulting companies

WESTERN CAROLINA UNIVERSITY
Natural Resources Management
Cullowhee, North Carolina

Fast Facts About the Program	Fast Facts About the School
• **Established:** 1985	• State-supported comprehensive coed institution
• **Enrollment:** 46	• 260-acre campus in rural setting
• **Faculty:** 3 (1 FT, 2 PT)	• **Enrollment:** 6,372
• **Student/Faculty Ratio:** 15:1	• **Faculty:** 443
• **Degrees Conferred Since Inception:** 49	• **Student/Faculty Ratio:** 16:1
• **Degrees Conferred in 1991:** 11	• **Tuition:** State resident: $676; nonresident: $5730
• **Contact:** Dr. Lawrence G. Kolenbrander, Coordinator, Natural Resources Management Program, Western Carolina University, Cullowhee, NC 28723; phone 704-227-7367	• **Fees:** $653
	• **Room and Board:** $2310
	• **Application Deadline:** 8/1
	• **Entrance Dfficulty Level:** Moderately difficult
	• **Contact:** Drumont Bowman, Director of Admissions, 704-227-7317

The Program

The program exists to provide undergraduate majors with instruction in an interdisciplinary, problem-solving approach to the conservation and utilization of the natural resources of America and the world. The program is heavily field-oriented and requires courses from a variety of disciplines

> **MAJOR/CONCENTRATIONS**
>
> **Natural Resources Management**
> Forest Resources Management
> Land Use Planning
> Water Resources Management

along with specific natural resources management courses. Students take 53 credit hours in general education and general elective classes; 54 credit hours of science, mathematics, and basic natural resources management courses; and 21 credit hours in the concentration. The program provides basic training in Geographic Information Systems (GIS) and computer mapping for all of its students. Majors are encouraged to participate in the many cooperative education opportunities available.

Special Features

The campus is within 30 miles of Great Smoky Mountains National Park and the Blue Ridge Parkway. Over 60% of the surrounding mountain lands are under ownership and management of the U.S. Forest Service. The Tennessee Valley Authority operates a large number of reservoirs in the region. Working relationships are maintained with these federal and additional state resource management agencies. The program has on-going student-designed and monitored research and demonstration studies in forest and water resources management on a 1,400 acre privately owned ranch in the area.

Who's Recruiting Who on Campus

Employers (Positions): U.S. Forest Service (Foresters, Forest Technicians, Recreation Specialists); U.S. Army Corps of Engineers (Resource Managers, Foresters); U.S. National Park Service (Interpretive Specialists, Resource Managers, Rangers/Law Enforcement); North Carolina State Forest Service (Foresters); Georgia State Parks and Recreation (Recreation and Resource Managers)

Glossary

ABET Accreditation Board for Engineering and Technology

acidity a measure of the effective concentration of hydrogen ions

acid rain rain that is more acid than normal because it contains sulfuric acid and nitric acid

adsorption adherence of a gas or liquid to the surface of a solid

aerobic requiring oxygen to live

alkalinity a measure of the amount of alkali in a substance or solution.

anaerobic able to live in the absence of oxygen

baling refuse a method of disposal in which refuse is compacted, fastened in bales (like hay), and deposited in a systematic order, reducing the amount of space needed for disposal

bioaccumulation the process of increasing biological concentration of a substance through links in a food chain; another term for biological magnification or biomagnification

biodegradable a compound that can be broken down into simpler compounds by microorganisms

biological magnification increased biological concentration of a substance through links in a food chain; biomagnification

blackwater domestic wastewater containing human body wastes

BOD Biological Oxygen Demand; a quantitative expression of the oxygen-depleting impact of a given amount of organic matter

Btu British thermal unit(s)

CAA Clean Air Act

CERCLA Comprehensive Environmental Response, Compensation, and Liability Act (Superfund Act), 1980, which provides funds for emergency cleanup of spills and abandoned or inactive hazardous waste sites

chlorinated hydrocarbons chemicals that contain specific arrangements of atoms of hydrogen, carbon, and chlorine; for example, the insecticides DDT and aldrin

COD Chemical Oxygen Demand; a quantitative expression of straight chemical oxygen depletion

cogeneration the use of waste energy from one energy-using process to drive another; for example, the use of waste incineration to generate steam for generating electricity

compactor a power-driven machine that compresses solid wastes and reduces their volume

compliance obeying all the federal and state regulations that apply

compost to decay; organic wastes partially decomposed by aerobic bacteria to an intermediate state

concentration the amount of one substance in a unit amount of another substance

consumption the measured amount of any resource or energy used in a given time by a given number of people

controlled incineration a process by which solid, liquid, or gaseous wastes are burned and changed into gases that are then cleaned before being discharged into the environment

corrosive causing the pH level to fall below 2 or above 12.5, or capable of dissolving or wearing away–especially of metals

DDT Dichlorodiphenyl trichloroethane (toxic insecticide)

DOT Department of Transportation

dump a site where mixed wastes are deposited without regard to protection of the environment

dumpster a large refuse container used by institutions, businesses, and multi-family dwellings to keep waste until it is collected by a sanitation department or other refuse-hauling service

ecological society a group of organisms and elements of the environment that operate in a natural cycle

ecology the relationship between organisms and their environment

energy recovery retrieval of energy from solid wastes by any conversion process; for example, heat produced by the burning of solid wastes

environment surroundings, indoors or out-of-doors

EPA Environment Protection Agency, 1970; the federal agency charged with the enforcement of all federal regulations having to do with environmental pollutants

exchange the use of waste from one activity for production in another activity

extraction the act or process of removing or separating; for example, metal from ore

FIFRA Federal Insecticides, Fungicides and Rodenticides Act; regulates use of toxic materials

flash point the temperature at which vapors ignite

food chain the set of organisms through which energy and materials progress through the various levels from producers to the highest consumers

fossil fuel a fuel derived from once-living matter; for example, coal, petroleum, or natural gas

fungicide a fungi killer

garbage food wastes; animal and vegetable wastes resulting from the handling, storage, sale, preparation, cooking, and serving of foods

GIS geographic information systems

graywater domestic wastewater containing other than human body wastes

groundwater water found in the porous spaces of soil and rock

hazardous materials or substances chemicals that pose a significant threat to human health and the environment

hazardous waste waste that is dangerous to human health or to the environment; toxic, corrosive, reactive, or ignitable chemicals

heavy metals metals such as cadmium, lead, and mercury that are persistent in the environment, are poisonous, and can be magnified in the food chain

herbicide a plant killer

humus a brown or black substance resulting from the partial decay of plant or animal matter

hygroscopic tending to take up water

illegal dumping disposing of waste in an unofficial location

impoundment a pool of water (lagoon) where liquid or semiliquid wastes are stored

incinerator a facility designed to reduce waste volume by burning, which turns the waste into gases and solids

industrial wastes scrap and solid wastes usually discarded from industrial operations or derived from the manufacturing process

infrastructure a substructure or underlying foundation; those facilities upon which a state or community depends; for example, roads, schools, power plants, and transportation

inorganic not composed of once-living material; for example, minerals

insecticide an insect killer

kwh kilowatt-hour

land disposal a method of depositing wastes on land; for example, a lagoon, open dump, or sanitary landfill

landfill a large outdoor area for waste disposal. (Landfills where waste is exposed to the atmosphere are called open dumps. Sanitary landfills are covered with soil)

LD Lethal Dose; the specific amount of a substance able to cause death

leachate liquid containing decomposed wastes, bacteria, and other materials that drains out of landfills

litter highly visible solid wastes that are generated by the consumer and carelessly discarded outside the regular disposal system

LULU Locally Unwanted Land Use; for example, jails, airports, and landfills

LUS Leaking Underground Storage; for example, leaking underground gasoline storage tanks

methane a colorless, odorless, flammable, gaseous hydrocarbon that is a product of the decomposition of organic matter, for example, produced in marshes and landfills and in collections of animal feces; CH_4

metric ton a measure of weight equal to 1,000 kilograms or 2,204.62 pounds

midnight dumping illegal disposal of hazardous waste

municipal waste the combined residential and commercial waste materials generated in a given municipal area

natural resources the supply of materials, not made by man, that is used for making goods

neutralization the process of destroying distinctive or active properties; for example, an alkali neutralizing an acid

NIMBY Not In My Backyard; refers to the fact that people want the convenience of necessary goods and proper waste disposal of those goods, provided the disposal area is not located near them

nonbiodegradable not able to be broken down by microorganism

nonrenewable not naturally restored or replenished

NPDES National Pollutant Discharge Elimination System

organic composed of living or once-living matter

OSHA Occupational Safety and Health Administration; regulates and sets the standards for health and safety practices in the workplace

particulate a small piece of solid matter or a droplet of liquid of a size that allows it to remain suspended in air

pathogen an organism that causes disease

PCB polychlorinated biphenyl; nonductor of electricity, used in transformers

percolate to pass a liquid gradually through small spaces or a porous substance; for example, rain passing through soil and waste in a landfill

persistent slowly or very slowly degradable in the environment; for example, glass and plastics

pesticide a pest (dandelion, fly, or corn-borer) killer

PET polyethylene terephthalate; a substance used, for example, for plastic soft drink bottles

petrochemical a chemical derived from petroleum or natural gas

pH the degree of acidity or alkalinity of a solution

planned obsolescence production of goods that become useless quickly so that more goods will have to be produced

pollution the contamination of soil, water, or the atmosphere by the discharge of wastes or other offensive materials

POTW Publicly Owned Treatment Works

RCRA Resource Conservation and Recovery Act, 1976; requires states to develop solid waste management plans and prohibits open dumps; identifies, lists, and sets the standard for hazardous wastes

RDF Refuse-Derived Fuel; the product obtained from the mechanical processing of municipal solid waste

reactive explosive

reclamation the restoration to a better or more useful state

recycle to separate a given waste material from other wastes and process it so that it can be used again in a form similar to its original use; for example, newspapers recycled into newspaper or cardboard

reduction the process of decreasing the amount of waste generated or replacing a hazardous substance with a safer one at each step of product development

renewable able to be restored or replenished; able to become new again

residue solid materials remaining after completion of a chemical or physical process, such as burning, evaporation, distillation, or filtration

resource something that can be used to make something else; for example, wood made into paper, iron ore into steel, bauxite into aluminum, sand into glass, old bottles into new ones, old newspapers into cardboard

resource recovery the taking of usable materials or energy from wastes; for example, paper incinerated to produce energy

rodenticide a rodent (rat, mouse) killer

rubbish solid wastes, excluding food wastes and ashes, taken from residences, commercial places, and institutions

sanitary landfill a land area where solid wastes are disposed of using a method that protects the environment by spreading the wastes in thin layers, compacting it to the smallest practical volume, and covering it with soil at the end of each working day

scrap solid wastes left over from construction or manufacturing and suitable for reprocessing

secure landfill a landfill designed to prevent the entry of water and the escape of leachate by the use of impermeable liners

sediment fine particles that do not dissolve easily or ever, whether suspended and settled

septic tank a domestic waste disposal system into which wastes are piped directly from the home; bacteria in the waste decompose the organic waste, sludge settles on the bottom of the tank, and effluent flows out into the ground through drains

sewage liquid and solid wastes carried off with water in sewers and drains

slag the fused refuse separated from a metal in the refining process

sludge mud, mire, or ooze covering the ground or forming a deposit at the bottom of bodies of water

solid waste any of a wide variety of solid materials, as well as some liquids in containers, which are discarded or rejected as being spoiled, useless, worthless, or in excess

solid waste management activities performed to get rid of waste produced in a community, including collecting, transporting, and processing

solvent a substance, usually a liquid, that can dissolve another substance

Superfund the fund established to implement the Comprehensive Environmental Response, Compensation, and Liability Act (CERCLA)

surface runoff precipitation that falls to the earth and flows by gravity to lower points

synthetic produced by a chemical process rather than of natural origin; man-made

throw-away society a society in which people buy things to use only one time or for a short period of time

tolerance the amount of variation allowed from a standard

toxic causing adverse physiological reactions at a given concentration

transfer station a place or facility where waste is taken from smaller trash collection vehicles and placed in larger ones for transporting to a disposal area

trash solid wastes, excluding food wastes, taken from residences, commercial places, and institutions, including both organic (e.g., plant trimmings and leaves) and inorganic materials

TSCA Toxic Substances Control Act, 1976; controls the production, distribution, and use of all potentially hazardous chemicals

TSDF Treatment Storage and Disposal Facility

virgin up to this time unused by man; occurring uncombined in its native form; for example, virgin silver

waste anything that is discarded, useless, or unwanted

waste generation the act or process of making wastes

waste management handling or controlling waste

waste processing acting upon discarded materials so they can be handled more easily (e.g., incineration) or so that resources can be recovered from them (e.g., recycling)

waste stream the series of wastes generated in the processes of production, utilization, and disposal of goods

wastewater water generated in the process of production in industrial, municipal, or sanitary use

Published with the permission of the Tennessee Valley Authority in Washington, DC.

Bibliography/
Resources

Bailey, Jill. *Gorilla Rescue.* Austin, Texas: Steck-Vaughn Library, 1990. Emmanual, an employee of the Rwandan National Park, saves several gorillas from poachers and sets out on a tracking expedition to count them for an upcoming census.

Basa, Nicholas. *Environmental Jobs for Scientists and Engineers.* New York: John Wiley and Sons Inc., 1992. Covers career opportunities in ten branches of engineering, including manufacturing, electronics, chemistry, biology, and computer science. Lists of professional and educational organizations and prospective employers and their addresses are also included.

Bennett, Steven J. *Ecoprenuering: The Complete Guide to Small Business Opportunities from the Environmental Revolution.* New York: John Wiley and Sons Inc., 1991. A sourcebook and start-up guide for anyone interested in becoming an environmental entrepreneur. Covers enterprises ranging from recycling to green travel services, discusses how to start a business, provides case studies, and lists sources of additional information.

Berger, John J. *Restoring the Earth.* New York: Alfred A. Knopf, 1985. Tells the true stories of dedicated individuals and groups who have worked or are now working to repair and restore the natural resources of the world.

Brooks, Paul. *Speaking for Nature.* Boston: Houghton-Mifflin Co., 1980. Chronicles the works of writers from Henry Thoreau to Rachel Carson to show how they have affected and shaped the movement to protect the American environment in the last century.

Brower, David. *Work In Progress.* Salt Lake City: Gibbs Smith Publisher, 1991. Brower, one of America's foremost environmentalists, describes some of the big issues that have defined his life's work as an activist. A founder of the Sierra Club, his roles have ranged from filmmaker to publisher and have spanned all issues concerning the well-being of the environment.

Bureau of Labor Statistics. *Occupational Outlook Handbook 1990-91.* Washington, D.C. U.S. Department of labor, 1990. A reference book, this volume describes a wide variety of careers. Includes information about the nature of the occupation, working conditions, qualification requirements, employment outlook, earnings, and related jobs as well as sources of additional information.

The CEIP Fund. *The Complete Guide to Environmental Careers.* Washington, D.C.: Island Press, 1989. Presents essential information needed to plan any career search, including salary levels, volunteer and internship opportunities, and entry-level requirements in the environmental field.

Day, David. *The Environmental Wars*. New York: St. Martin's Press, 1989. Offers an impassioned look at true stories from the battle to save the earth. With tales from individuals and groups, the book outlines how today's environmental challenges are being met.

DeBlieu, Jan. *Meant to be Wild: The Struggle to Save Endangered Species through Captive Breeding*. Golden, Colorado: Fulcrum Publications, 1991. The story of the struggle by scientists and conservationists to capture and then release wild animals into their natural world in an effort to avoid their becoming extinct.

Embery, Joan and Denise Demong. *My Wild World*. New York: Delacorte Press, 1980. The story of the famous San Diego Zoo's Wild Animal Ambassador. Embery tells of her life's work of caring for, training, and living with animals.

Fanning, Odom. *Opportunities in Environmental Careers*. Lincolnwood, Illinois: VGM Career Horizons, 1991. Covers a wide variety of jobs in the environmental field. Provides an overview of the field, employment outlook, advancement opportunities, educational requirements, and salaries and sources of additional information. Additional titles in the *Opportunities In* series include specific information on careers in forestry, marine/maritime, recreation, engineering, chemistry, biology, energy, agriculture, and other environmentally relevant subjects.

Foster, Rory C. *Dr. Wildlife*. New York: Franklin Watts, 1985. Recounts the tale of veterinarian Foster, from his first encounter treating an injured fawn to the struggle with launching the Northwoods Wildlife Hospital and Rehabilitation Center.

Hawes, Gene R. and Douglass L. Brownstone. *The Outdoor Careers Guide*. New York: Facts on File, 1986. Offers a practical, systematic approach to selecting, training for, and succeeding in an outdoor career. Covers educational requirements, salary levels, and advancement opportunities, has profiles of the fifty hottest outdoor careers, and explains how to find and get a job.

Hayes, Harold T.P. *The Dark Romance of Dian Fossey*. New York: Simon and Schuster, 1990. Recounts the incredible life of Dian Fossey, who lived with and studied the last remaining mountain gorillas of Africa. Not a scientist by trade, Fossey learned more about the mountain gorilla than anyone who came before her.

Hopke, William E., ed. *Encyclopedia of Careers and Vocational Guidance–Vol. 2 Professional Careers*. Chicago: J. G. Ferguson Publishing Co., 1990. A reference book, this volume provides a brief description of professional careers, covering definition, history, nature of the work, educational requirements, opportunities, related occupations, outlook, and earnings and lists sources of additional information.

Janovy, John Jr. *On Becoming a Biologist*. New York: Harper and Row, 1983. Written by a naturalist and teacher, the book explores the field of biology. Covers the actual practice of biology, teaching and learning biology, the practical aspects of biology as a career, and the role of biologists in the well-being of humans and the environment.

Jasperson, William. *A Day in the Life of a Marine Biologist.* Boston: Little, Brown and Co., 1982. Follows a day in the life of Dr. Arthur Humes, a marine biologist who discovered new ocean animals in the earth's major bodies of water.

LaBastille, Anne. *Assignment: Wildlife.* New York: E. P. Dutton, 1980. LaBastille, a conservationist, writer, and ecological consultant, describes her adventures ranging from saving an endangered species in Guatemala to establishing a wildlife preserve in the Caribbean.

LaMay, Craig L. and Everette E. Dennis, eds. *Media and the Environment.* Washington, D.C.: Island Press, 1991. Explores media coverage of environmental issues. Media professionals, editors, broadcast producers, and writers answer controversial questions about how the media cover the environment.

Lee, Sally. *The Throwaway Society.* New York: Franklin Watts, 1990. Examines the growing problem of how to handle solid wastes, exploring areas such as collecting and transporting waste, sanitary landfills, incineration, recycling, and ocean dumping.

Mainstream Access Inc. *The Energy Job Finder.* Englewood Cliffs, New Jersey: Prentice Hall Inc., 1981. Describes careers in oil, gas, coal, and nuclear and solar energy. Includes job descriptions, earnings, and hints for getting into the field.

Norman, Charles. *John Muir: Father of Our National Parks.* New York: Julian Messner, 1987. Recounts the life of John Muir, world-famous naturalist, geologist, writer, and explorer who led the fight to establish what is today the national park system.

Poynter, Margaret. *The Zoo Lady: Belle Benchley and the San Diego Zoo.* New York: Dillon Publishing Co., 1980. Presents the twenty-five-year career of Belle Benchley as the director of the San Diego Zoo, which began with a temporary job as bookkeeper.

Pringle, Laurence. *Restoring Our Earth.* Hillside, New Jersey: Enslow Publishers Inc., 1987. Describes the efforts being made by professionals and volunteers to restore the damaged condition of the earth, from rebuilding marshes to replanting woodlands.

Pringle, Laurence P. *Saving Our Wildlife.* Hillside, New Jersey: Enslow Publishers Inc., 1990. Explains the importance of wildlife and the ways in which people are trying to save various species in North America.

Reisner, Marc. *Game Wars: The Undercover Pursuit of Wildlife Poachers.* New York: Viking Penguin, 1991. A firsthand account of how undercover game wardens operate and the covers they devise, including the subterfuge and lies needed to pull off a successful sting operation. This is the true story of wildlife cops and the outlaws they stalk.

Riccuite, Edward R. *The Work with Wildlife: Jobs for People Who Want to Work with Animals.* New York: Harper and Row, 1983. Introduces various jobs that involve working with wildlife, including game warden, nature writer, and field biologist.

Rinard, Judith E. *Wildlife, Making a Comeback: How Humans Are Helping.* Washington, D.C.: The National Geographic Society, 1987. Focuses on previously endangered species that have made comebacks and avoided extinction on account of world efforts made toward wildlife conservation.

Rossbacher, Lisa A. *Career Opportunities in Geology and the Earth Sciences.* New York: Arco Publishing, Inc., 1983. Explains everything you need to know about a career in earth sciences. Included are job descriptions, educational requirements, potential salaries, working conditions, and addresses of professional organizations and college geology departments.

Shapiro, Stanley Jay. *Exploring Careers in Science.* New York: The Rosen Publishing Group, Inc., 1989. Explores what scientists really do, where they work, their income potential, and educational requirements and how to pick the area of science best suited to you. Fields covered range from conservation sciences to environmental sciences.

Tessar, Jenny E. *The Waste Crisis.* New York: Facts on File, 1991. Examines all kinds of waste, including commercial, industrial, toxic, and radioactive. Discusses the problems and possible solutions connected with the existence and management of waste pollutants.

Wild, Russell, ed. *The Earth Care Annual 1990.* Emmaus, Pennsylvania: Rodale Press, 1990. Reporting from around the world regarding what individuals and groups can and are doing to protect the environment. Issues covered range from acid rain to wildlife.

Geographical Index

Index of Colleges and Universities